# Counter-Terrorism

## *Narrative Strategies*

## Ajit Maan

University Press of America,® Inc.

Lanham • Boulder • New York • Toronto • Plymouth, UK

**Copyright © 2015 by University Press of America,® Inc.**
4501 Forbes Boulevard, Suite 200, Lanham, Maryland 20706
UPA Aquisitions Department (301) 459-3366

Unit A, Whitacre Mews, 26-34 Stannary Street,
London SE11 4AB, United Kingdom

British Library Cataloguing in Publication Information Available

Library of Congress Control Number: 2014953415
ISBN: 978-0-7618-6498-1 (cloth : alk. paper)—ISBN: 978-0-7618-6499-8 (electronic)
ISBN: 978-0-7618-6775-3 (pbk : alk. paper)

The author gratefully acknowledges permission to reprint "Calls to Terror and Other
Weak Narratives" (forthcoming) by Ajit Maan, in Narrative and Conflict: Explorations in
Theory and Practice, issue 2, 2014
and
"Post-Colonia Practices and Narrative Nomads" by Ajit Maan, in Sikh Formations: Religion, Culture, Theory, December 2005 Routledge. Reprinted by permission of the publish-
er Taylor & Francis Ltd. http://www.tandf.co.uk/journals.

This book is dedicated to my father,

Dr. Shivcharan Singh Maan,

who impressed me long ago with the exceptional powers of narrative.

# Contents

*Chapter One*

# Introduction

*Seduction and Other Narrative Dangers*

Narratives are powerful. And their power is tricky. They can illuminate, manipulate, inspire, entertain, blame, seduce, or provide an alibi. Narratives are never neutral. Their very nature is strategic. There is no narrative that is devoid of strategy. Narrative is a rendering of events, actions, and characters in a certain way for a certain purpose. The purpose is persuasion. The method is identification.

Understanding and harnessing the persuasive powers of narrative is central to U.S. and international counter-terrorism efforts. There is general agreement that there is an urgent need to destabilize and exploit weaknesses in terrorist recruitment narratives while simultaneously developing effective counter-terrorism narratives.

Imperative questions to ask whenever one encounters a persuasive narrative are: Whose narrative is this? What power(s) does it serve? What and who does it legitimate and what and who does it suppress? What are its strategic techniques and how do they operate?

The chapters that comprise this book ask those questions of dangerous narratives: contemporary narratives, narratives we hear every day, narratives we are a part of, narratives we confront, and narratives in need of a re-write.

"Calls to Terror and Other Weak Narratives" addresses two related persuasive powers— narrative identification and trajectory— and demonstrates how certain types of compositional structures lend themselves to manipulation and leave audiences vulnerable to manipulation. That vulnerability cuts both ways. It is essential from a security standpoint that we get ahead of it, understand how it works, and turn it around.

"Deconstructing Pathologizing Narratives: Questioning the Truth Status of Constructed Ideas" first deconstructs the persuasive power of exemplary contemporary calls to terrorist violence by uncovering strategies that create the illusion that political ideologies are a reflection of natural phenomena, and secondly, analyzes techniques that encourage (mis)identification.

"Psychological Warfare: Colonizing Narratives as Recruitment Strategy" makes a connection unique to studies in terrorism; it is a connection between techniques of colonization and techniques in terrorist recruitment. In both cases narrative is used to naturalize and normalize politically motivated ideologies. And in both cases narrative identification encourages individuals to take actions contrary to their best interests. I refer to these techniques as forms of psychological warfare. They operate without the implementation of physical force, without the continual presence of an external oppressor, and their effects are insidious: they are continued internally.

While diasporic populations, particularly of the second and third generation, are often targets of terrorist recruiters, "Post-Colonial Practices and Narrative Nomads" demonstrates that diasporias are in a unique position resulting from familiarity with the conceptual systems of two or more cultures that should enable resilience to coercive narratives. A new American narrative should encourage this type of ironic positioning (Haraway, 1991): holding together incompatible values and ideas because both are necessary and true.

The potential incompatibility of cultural conceptual systems, I argue in "Beyond Common Ground," should not be regarded as problematic if we understand narrative as structurally bigger, better, stronger and smarter than that of a singular Master narrative. The largely metaphorical nature of cognition, the centrality of the receiver of communication in meaning-making, and the importance of narrative in both *creating* and addressing conflict, should have a bearing on the development of counter-terrorist strategies and in the development of a new American narrative.

That being said, creating an effective counter-terrorist narrative is only half the narrative workload. Director of the Terrorism Research Initiative, Alex Schmid (2014), makes a crucial point about the need for division between counter-narrative and alternative narrative. Both are necessary. Each has a different job.

A strategic counter-narrative addresses a terrorist narrative on its own terms. It will question, undermine, and deconstruct the way the narrative problematic is formulated. It will expose logical fallacies, false dichotomies and metaphoric manipulation. It will raise the voices of the silenced. And it will expose the political interests of the powers that generate and perpetuate terrorist narratives.

The alternative narrative, however, should not directly address the terrorist narrative. Instead it should present an alternative that doesn't define itself by recourse to the problem as defined and framed by terrorists. Otherwise, we limit ourselves to playing by someone else's rules within someone else's narrative. The only sense in which an alternative narrative should be mindful of the terrorist narratives is to be careful not to repeat its weaknesses. As I will demonstrate, this is not an easy task and requires a willingness to examine the regulatory functions of our own frames of reference. As Dan McAdams (2008) observed, "Knowing who we are as Americans should involve knowing the strengths and limitations of the stories we live by, and knowing that others may live by stories very different from our own." An example of the stories others live by are tragedies. Our own narratives would be enriched by an understanding of the narrative power of tragedy (McAdams, 2008, Alon and Omar, 2004) in which fate, chance, and luck, work together with human agency to render a more morally complex narrative.

I will argue in favor of a more complex narrative *structure* and will argue that one limitation of the stories we live by is what we assume about how a story should proceed, "…the plot's redemptive features and its emphasis on the protagonist's forward progress are staples of a distinctively American narrative heritage." Narrative conventions are only conventions: they are culturally conditioned ways of telling a good story.

Terrorists use the conventional Master narrative and it has been persuasive. It will continue to be persuasive until it is challenged. This book represents just such a challenge. And it represents a unique challenge: a post-colonial structuralist one. I will demonstrate how the form or structure of narrative determines its content. Conventions of storytelling are also conventions about what is included in a story and what is not. Alternative narratives should avoid making the same mistake (a mistake we have been making) and instead we should "complicate" (Zalman 2009) a fundamental Master narrative (our own and others') with multiple narratives.

A central theme throughout this work is that a single unified "Master Narrative" is, despite its disguise, vulnerable to exploitation and should be avoided in favor of a richer more complex narrative structure. The National Coordinator of Counter-Terrorism in the Netherlands summarized the consensuses of scholars, government officials, and terrorism experts at a conference on countering violent extremist narratives at The Hague, concerning precisely this point, "…it was deemed impossible and unwise for Western governments to aspire to control and employ a central counter-narrative" (instead they should) "promote multiple narratives" Erik Akerboom (2010).

This work does not attempt to treat the phenomena of terrorism in general, defined for the scope of this book as politically motivated violent and illegal use of force and intimidation against civilian populations intended to gain publicity (Schmid 2012), rather, this book specifically addresses recruitment narratives. State sponsored terrorism is also beyond the scope of this work. Note also that I am specifically focused on potential targets of terrorist recruitment *within* the United States. And when I refer to terrorism and the danger of domestic recruitment, I refer to the threat posed by the likes of Al Qaeda and ISIS, as well as to the equal if not greater threat to national security posed by right-wing separatist groups within the United States. Having thus limited my focus, let me add that this book is more than an academic treatment of terrorist narratives. This book *is* a counter-terrorist narrative that confronts terrorist recruitment narratives head-on.

*Chapter Two*

# Calls to Terror
# and Other Weak Narratives

## INTRODUCTION

Understanding and harnessing the persuasive powers of narrative is central to current U.S. counter-terrorism efforts. There is general agreement that there is an urgent need to develop effective counter-terrorism narratives while simultaneously destabilizing and exploiting weaknesses in terrorist recruitment narratives. This chapter addresses two related persuasive powers—narrative identification and trajectory—and uncovers structural weaknesses that can be strategically manipulated.

The role of narrative is recognized as so crucial to counter-terrorism efforts that the Office of Naval Research has funded a research project designed to study its persuasive effects, called "Identifying and Countering Islamist Extremist Narratives" (2009) to investigate how, among other effects, cultural narratives can be used to further ideological agendas. The Defense Advanced Research Projects Agency has funded research designed to study the neurobiology of narrative comprehension, test narrative theories, and determine the connection between narrative and persuasion (2012). Previously the domain of the Humanities, this project attempts to find empirical evidence for narrative theories by engaging multi-modal neuroimaging in the interest of discovering the neural networks involved in narrative comprehension and persuasion, and to determine how the structural components of narrative can induce or disrupt narrative understanding. The Rand Corporation's presentation "Strategic Narratives: Their Uses and Limitations" (2011) to the US Advisory Commission on Public Diplomacy, was guided by essential questions about the form and function of narrative: the elements and characteristics of narratives, the ownership and control of narratives, and narrative conflict.

From the Naval Postgraduate School, William Casebeer and James Russell insist,

> failure on our part to come to grips with the narrative dimensions of the war on terrorism is a weakness already exploited by groups such as Al Qaeda; we can fully expect any adaptive adversary to act quickly to fill story gaps and exploit weaknesses in our narrative…(Casebeer and Russell, 2005, p. 3).

And as NATO spokesman Mark Laity has said,

> …a constant weakness in our information campaigns is the weakness of our narratives… Our opponents, terrorists, often do better at this than us. They tap into culture, national myths, and prejudices, and differing value systems…To succeed in the long-term we need to tap into narratives… (Laity, 2009)

Because most of us are not conscious of the power of narrative, narrative is even more powerful. It is a tool that we can use, and if we don't it will use us. We are being used by someone's narrative as we sit here now. If we think about narrative at all, most of us tend to think about the theme – what the narrative is about. Narrative structure, on the other hand, is generally assumed. And when we assume something we do so uncritically. I would like to turn a critical eye to what is accepted as standard narrative form and its implications.

## STRUCTURE DETERMINES CONTENT

Narratives can be weaker or stronger, more persuasive or less persuasive, depending upon the effectiveness of both the formal elements and the metaphorical reference. In this chapter I focus on two central features of narrative persuasiveness: formal structure, because form affects function, and identification, because identification influences action.

In this context I am using story and narrative interchangeably. When I refer to a story or a narrative I am referring, as Aristotle did in the *Poetics*, to an artfully arranged telling of events for the purpose of persuasion. This is distinct from a "history," or a simple litany of events.

We all have narratives, and we all act in relation to the narrative we see ourselves as a part of, but we don't all share the same structural assumptions. That means there is no universal cross-cultural agreement about how a story should proceed. As McAdams (2008) observes, "Our stories spell out our identities. But they also speak to and for culture. Life stories sometimes say as much about the culture wherein they are told as they do about the teller of the story." (p. 1)

Most of our contemporaries concerned with terrorism and narrative begin by making an assumption about what narrative is—an assumption about its form or structure. For example, Casebeer and Russell assert that narratives generally have a beginning, middle, and an end. Citing Gustav Freytag (Freytag's Triangle), and Joseph Campbell's study of the structure of myths, they relate a structure familiar to western audiences, "there is some beginning, a problem presents itself that leads to a climax, which resolves itself into an ending" (p.4). They follow a long tradition of assumptions about narrative form. It is an assumption familiar to lay persons and academics alike, and it has its foundation in Aristotle's *Poetics,*

Now a whole is that which has a beginning, middle, and end. A beginning is that which is not itself necessarily after any-thing else, and which has naturally something else after it; an end is that which is naturally after something itself, either as its necessary or usual consequent, and with nothing else after it; and a middle, that is by nature after one thing and has also another after it. A well-constructed plot, therefore, cannot either begin or end at any point one likes; beginning and end in it must be of the forms just described (Janko trans. 1987).

Aristotle's poetic structure has become the norm for the way narratives are structured. That structure has the following elements: it is *linear* (goes from beginning to middle to end) and is *unified* (there is a theme into which each component part plays a role) and is *temporally ordered* (time is an essential feature in the structuring operation). It is important to recognize the non-universality of Western narrative structure so we don't make the mistake of projecting a culturally specific assumption onto those who don't share it, and so we are aware of the ways in which it can be exploited and can be used to exploit.

While there is general agreement that narrative is both expressive and constitutive of identity (Ricoeur, 1995, 1992; Johnson, 1993; MacIntyre, 1981; Lloyd, 1993; Schaffer, 1992; Bateson, 1990; Bruner, 1990; Linde, 1993) many contemporary philosophers, literary theorists, and psychologists have argued, at length, for the centrality of the classical Western narrative structure because they link a unified linear narrative, in the form just described, to identity. But they link it not to just to any kind of identity; they link it to coherent unified identity in particular,

It is indeed in the story recounted, with its qualities of unity, internal structure, and completeness which are conferred by emplotment, that the character preserves throughout the story an identity correlative to that of the story itself...How, indeed, could a subject of action give an ethical character to his or her own life taken as a whole, if this life were not gathered in some way, and how could this not occur if not, precisely, in the form of a narrative? (Ricoeur, 1992)

In his classic text, *Acts of Meaning* (1990), psychologist Jerome Bruner insists, "What gives the story its unity is the manner in which plight, characters, and consciousness interact to yield a structure that has a start, a development, and a sense of an ending." Narrative, according to Bruner, has four grammatical constituents: agency, linearity, canonicality, and perspective (p. 77).

Most people would agree that three of four of these constituents are not neutral but rather reflect interest. Those three are: are agency, canonicality, and perspective. I think the fourth, linearity, is not neutral either although linearity deceptively masquerades as neutral so its resulting persuasive power goes undetected. (Maan, 2013) As Bruner says, "the meaning of what happened is strictly determined by the order and form of its sequence" (p. 90). It is imperative to recognize that "the meaning of what happened" can be manipulated by enlisting an ancient fallacy that linear narrative form relies upon for its enormous persuasive power; it is the "post hoc ergo propter hoc" (after this, therefore because of this) logical fallacy. As McAdams and McLean (2013) have pointed out, in recent studies of narrative identity researchers have focused on psychological adaptation and development but more needs to be done to "disentangle causal relations between features of life stories." Narratives convey a specific understanding of the events they are about. And this understanding involves a particular way of organizing events. And in this way, narrative, by its very nature, is strategic and its strategic nature is inseparable from its form. Narrative bestows meaning on what were previously just a series of events that are sometimes related and sometimes not related. It ties together events in a certain way for a certain purpose. Narratives have "rhetorical aims or illocutionary intentions that are not merely expository, but rather, partisan." They work to "cajole, to deceive, to flatter, to justify" (Bruner, p. 85– 86). And its formal elements effect action "what you do is drastically effected by how you recount what you are doing, will do, or have done" (Bruner, p. 87).

Narrative is a way to appropriate, or to give meaning to, experience, and in the context of this discussion, involuntary aspects of experience are essential (note that many calls to violence first begin with casting the potential terrorist as a victim). I may not have control over my environment and circumstances but narrative gives me control over how I understand my environment and my circumstances. We re-create ourselves with the stories we tell, that is, events happen but we determine the status of those events in our narratives. In classical western narrative, the meaning of present events, past events, and future action, conforms to certain principles of emplotment. The event or action is going to fit either into the initial stage (harmony) or the second stage (conflict) or the last stage (resolution).

The application of his poetic structure to autobiography (individual identity) and cultural narrative (group identity) is not what Aristotle intended, however, that lack of intention is not itself problematic (ideas don't have to be used as prescribed to be useful or not). The problems that result from this unintended application are:

1. The exclusive application of Aristotelian poetic structure, to the exclusion of any other restricts information content.
2. The structure and the meaning of action is therefore similarly constricted.
3. Forms of narrative, identity, and action that are inconsistent with Aristotelian structure are not recognized or mis-identified.

Classical Western narrative structure is a foundational myth that has served a purpose and continues to be useful but emergent sensibilities are overly restricted by it. Linear narrative restricts reframing by restricting the structure of the new narrative to the culturally sanctioned structure of the old one, so that there will be a new theme but it will be coerced into the same structure with all the same attendant problems and we are back in the business of gathering together experiences that cohere with the dominant theme and editing life of its exceptions and inconsistencies. The only way that experience of chance, luck, accident, or tragedy enter in is if they *are* the dominant theme.

A few theorists have pointed to the handicap that this narrative structure places on the identity formation. Psychologist Roy Schaffer, for example, describes problems that occur when multiplicities of experience are diminished and reduced in order to represent a consistent self which can fit into a unified and whole culturally imposed narrative structure,

> ...self-deception is but one instance of a set of problematic ideas that are introduced by self theorists or grand self narratives. It is advantageous to regard self-deception as a story that people tell in order to present themselves or make a psychoanalytic interpretation .... It is a story that 'works': it communicates effectively and it helps construct experience. *But it is only one version*" (Schaffer, 1992). (The emphasis is mine.)

And philosopher Rosi Braidotti fears the normative force of this structure, "I am struck by the violence of the gesture that binds a fractured self to the performative illusion of unity.... and by its incomprehensible force" (Braidotti, 1994).

One of the concerns of Steve Corman and other strategic communication scholars is to restore lost U.S. credibility while keeping in mind that Western notions of credibility may not translate (Corman, Trethewey, Goodall, Lang, 2008). I want to add that an essential aspect of credibility that may not translate is the value of unified selfhood and the attendant association with credibility in the Western mind. The self-consistency associated with Western ideals of credible selfhood may not translate. Conversely the lack of self-consistency may not be universally perceived as a threat to credibility. This is a good thing from a strategic perspective as it allows for changes in policy without threatening credibility.

If, as those of us who argue for the centrality of narrative understanding insist, identity and action are correlative to narrative, and if unity-wholeness-linearity are not universal characteristics of narrative, then they are also not universal characteristics of identity or the actions that result from it (them).

And this is good news for counter-terrorism strategists. Alternative narrative structures leave more room for changes and re-association and re-framing.

It is possible to be inconsistent without any threat to identity. So while one with a traditional narrative orientation will think of himself or herself as the same consistent self no matter where he goes or when he exists in time, another person with a less rigid narrative orientation may think in terms of various aspects of self in various contexts at various times, and this sort of orientation is not understood as a threat to the stability of selfhood because consistency and uniqueness are not universally recognized central features of selfhood. What to some may seem to be a "talking out of both sides of one's mouth" may in fact be a rational and functionally obvious way of being in different contexts, with competing demands, at different times.

If we remove our uni-narrative blinders, we can welcome an American narrative that would function as an anti-terrorism narrative by offering and exemplifying a more attractive alternative that is inclusive of change and multiplicity. This narrative strategy would create conflict in the mind of the potential recruit, not by listing all the counter-facts and counter-examples to the terrorist narrative (as that would be engaging the conflict) but rather by offering an alternative that does not threaten any sense of self by requiring individuals to make the types of choices that fundamentalist narratives attempt to force their audience to make.

## ANTI-TERRORISM STRATEGY

Nothing is as persuasive as a story. There is no form of argument, no logical process that can move us the way a story does, because stories encourage us to identify. Who one sees oneself as, and the story one sees oneself as a part of, both compel action consistent with the self story. And if the narrative form privileges "unity" and "wholeness" then identity and the actions that result from it will be consistent with this form. What is the problem with that? One problem is that identity, whether personal or group, will be made up of consistent experience. Only the experience that fits into a whole and unified form is included in the narrative. The form doesn't admit anomalous experience or action. There is no room for exceptions to the dominant story line. And as philosopher/novelist Rebecca Goldstein (1989) warns "the aesthetic preference for wholeness will often lead us to actions we would not otherwise undertake." (p. 57)

The over-emphasis on self-consistency is incongruent with change brought by changes in external circumstances, or changes occurring as a result of time passing, or changes brought about by critical reflection, or from gaining new information. The problem with understanding a self as that being who narrates a whole and unified story, a story with one dominant authorial voice and consciousness, linearly over time, is that potentially meaningful experience will be left out of a unified and whole plot structure if it is anomalous or if it cannot be synthesized. Experience will be dichotomized as meaningful/trivial, anomaly/pattern, and will be included or repressed depending upon which category it falls into.

Culturally varied and contextually specific ways of being are at odds with a consciousness directed toward discovering, or creating, unity between diverse phenomena and its attendant orientation toward inner integration and consistency. That sort of orientation can cause acute problems in situations of narrative conflict. Because cultural and ideological conflict is inevitable it is strategically pragmatic to negotiate a narrative framework that is not threatened by change.

I would like to refer back to the claim made by the title of this chapter. A unified/whole/sequential narrative is a narrative that can be easily manipulated and easily be manipulating. Al-Qaeda (Schmid 2014) and other terrorist groups have manipulated it very effectively. A narrative with one theme, a fundamentalist narrative, silences information that is consistent or contrary to the theme. What makes a fundamentalist narrative structure tactically manipulating? There are several things:

1. temporal order (because simply switching the order of events will alter moral responsibility),
2. unity or coherence (because this type of narrative leaves no room for anomalies or exceptions or change)
3. linearity (because all current events fit into the middle which is the conflict stage. The end is only projected and there will be endless disagreement about when the "beginning" was, for example, did the war on terror begin after Sept 11 or years before?)

## Chapter Three

# Deconstructing Pathologizing Narratives

*Questioning the Truth Status of Constructed Ideas*

## INTRODUCTION

As a philosopher with interests in narrative and identity, I approach the problem of terrorism not, as some might assume, to propose an alternative ideology, but rather, to identify and challenge the techniques dominating ideologies use to incite individuals and groups to act in accordance with them. Those techniques involve the strategic mis-use of narrative identity. Pathologizing narratives are narratives that tell a story about what is wrong and locate what is wrong inside an individual (White, 1990).

Pathologizing narratives are narratives that encourage individual audience members to internalize the description of diseased social/political situation. The description of social ills as diseased is itself dubious and the personalization of that description is even more suspect. A textual comparative analysis and deconstruction of two exemplary pathologizing narratives reveals logical fallacies, strategically neglected perspectives, and moral contraband.

Colonizing narratives are narratives that recruit individuals to play an active role in their own subjugation (Maan, 2005). Separately these types of narratives are dangerous. Combined they have been lethal.

Pathologizing narratives will be the subject of this chapter and colonizing narratives will be the subject of the next. I will begin with a definition and description of pathologizing narrative, provide several examples, proceed to a textual analysis and deconstruction of exemplary pathologizing narratives that will involve uncovering logical fallacies, voicing exceptions to the dominant narrative, and identifying narrative contraband— elements that the texts import under the radar.

## DEFINITION

A pathologizing narrative is a narrative with a theme that something is wrong and the thing that is wrong is inside a person. One of Michael White's examples goes like this: A parent brings a teenager to therapy because the teen is "irresponsible." The parent proceeds to tell the therapist a narrative which includes only supporting evidence despite the fact that, upon examination, it turns out that the instances in which the teen acted responsibly far outnumber the instances of irresponsible behavior. The parent has been disturbed by some behavior, has decided on a label or a theme, and collects and narrates supporting evidence while omitting events and actions that do not fit or contribute to the theme. The teenager, in turn, identifies with the story he is told about himself (after all it has his name on it) and if not for intervention, continues the collection and narration of events and actions that fit the theme and he disregards all that do not fit the theme and even provides more narrative material through more irresponsible behavior.

The parents' Master narrative is titled "Irresponsible." The Master narrative in most terrorist calls to violence is titled "Victim." In just the same way the teenager internalizes the Master narrative of his parents and acts accordingly, in order for terrorist narratives to take hold, the target audience has to internalize victim status so that they will act accordingly. Ironically, and often, neither the authors of the terrorist manifestos, nor the intended audiences, are direct victims (Volkan, 2012). Consider, for example, the Boston marathon bombers who internalized victim status when neither was victimized personally. White would say they were under the influence of a narrative titled "Victimization."

Victims, however, do not write manifestos. Victims do not detonate explosive devices in crowds. Even if one has been a victim in the past, victim status is not static. Once a victim uses power she has access to the same choices anyone the same possessing power has. Having been victimized, either directly or indirectly can, however, according to psychiatrist Vamik Volkan, cause psychological regression in both individuals and large groups. Two basic techniques in "The 'education' of Suicide Bombers," (1997) are, first, "trainers" find young people who have been traumatized such that they develop "cracks" in their personal identities and then they fill those cracks with large group identity. They are then agents of large group identity, which they feel is under attack, "Killing one's self (and one's personal identity) and 'others' (enemies) doesn't matter. What matters is that the act of bombing (terrorism) brings self-esteem and attention to the large-group identity" (7).

## EXAMPLES OF PATHOLOGIZING NARRATIVES

Let us proceed by examining two conflict saturated narratives, each a call to global violence. Following the examples I will make a brief detour through logical analysis, looking for internal inconsistencies and confusions and logical fallacies, however, the logical fallacies of narrative calls to violence, even when called out, will be

irrelevant to their persuasive power, and impotent against pathologizing powers.

My primary concern in this chapter is to examine the way in
which this type of narrative, as the name suggests, does not *find*
something wrong; it *makes* something wrong. It makes something
wrong by instituting a Master narrative titled "Victim." The linear,
sequential structure then variously omits and centralizes information consistent with the theme and then locates the "victim" inside
the intended audience.

I have chosen the two texts, "Intro Material for People New to
Stormfront" (Stormfront.org) and a World Islamic Front Statement,
"Jihad Against Jews and Crusaders" (February 23, 1998), because
they are representative, in both form and content, of the type of
strategic communication employed by extremist groups. The structure, and the persuasive power of it, will by now be familiar to the
reader. It goes something like this:

> In the beginning, We, our people, lived in utopia (note that
> utopia is usually associated with natural abundance, racial
> homogeny, self-regulation) until the "others" came (this is the
> conflict stage) bringing with them all sorts of bad things (other
> religions, immoral practices, all associated with unnatural phe-
> nomena) and we and our way of life were overcome. The "oth-
> ers" took over (often a literal or at least metaphoric reference to
> the rape of the land accompanies this description). This is where
> we are now—in the middle of the story. It can go either way. It
> is up to you, the audience, to determine which way this story
> will end. If you do nothing, the end of the story will resemble
> the middle. But in an alternatively projected future we can expel
> the enemy, take back our lands, teach our children our old ways,
> and decontaminate our selves and our land of all forms of multi-
> plicity. And we must do this in such a way that we are never
> threatened again. The story of our victimization must not repeat
> itself.

## TEXTUAL ANALYSIS

Keeping in mind the work that structure does, let us break down the component parts of the content of both narratives. The Stormfront text is divided into four parts, the "Introduction," "The Nature of the Problem," "A Warning About Jewish Tactics," and "What You Can Do To Help Save Yourself, Your People and the World."

1. The Introduction does two things: it contextualizes this narrative within the Obama presidency, and then raises the issue of strategy, that is, "what works (i.e., gets Whites to see and accept the reality we face)." This is followed by a litany of potential strategic narrative content that various white separatists think will be persuasive, for example, some think religion can be persuasive, others don't. Some think the narrative should center upon "negative behavior of blacks" while others think the focus should be the "positive aspects of White Western civilization." In the end of this section the author describes himself as a "lover of truth" who will not merely reflect what others want him to say. In other words, the audience is being told that the writer considered various manipulative strategies and concluded that he would implement no strategy. The writer announces that the audience is about to hear the truth un-strategically announced.

2. In the second part of the narrative, "The Nature of the Problem" has four assertions: a) The "problem" is inside individuals. The problem is biological rather than ideological. b) The future will be "unfair" if action isn't taken by the audience. c) The prime directive : reservations for "Whites" should be created. d) The "us" and "them" categories positions unindoctrinated "Whites" into the "them" category.

3. There is a reiteration of the theme of internalizing what is described as the problem, "(the problem) is not ideology, it is blood.... Blacks and Mexicans don't have the minds to main-

tain White man's social, cultural, and economic systems."
The narrative continues, "Most Whites" know that if the U.S.
and Europe are "flooded" with "Browns and Blacks" the
quality of life for Whites will decrease and that is "not fair."
The explanation for how things have become "so grave" for
Whites is that : "It was the Jews." They have apparently been
"working behind the scenes" to "rule the world." The problem with Jews, like "Browns and Blacks" is their blood, because "as a race they suffer from psychopathy." The definition of psychopathy is conveniently provided for us: "a mental disorder whose (sic) main symptoms is the ability to lie
like there is no tomorrow." This is followed by the "prime
directive": "We must secure the existence of our people and a
future for White children. We want a few areas on the Earth
(and states in the U.S.) that are reserved for Whites and
Whites only." The audience is then told that the "attentive
reader" will wonder how the situation for Whites has become
so "grave" and how "some Whites" have become so "detached from reality" as to believe the "delusion of racial
equality." Whites who don't buy what this author is selling
are told they are not in the majority and are "inattentive,"
"detached from reality," "delusional," not "in their right
mind," "traitors," and "cowards." The narrative proceeds, in
the third part, to provide Biblical citations in the form of "tid
bits" of "facts" for the forgoing assertions.

4. The last section of this narrative is a call to action in the now
   familiar form: take action and change the course of the future
   otherwise your victimization and that of "our people" will
   continue.

Let's break down the Jihad narrative the same way. Its component fifteen paragraphs are comprised of the following:

1. There is a prime directive, "slay the pagans," followed by a threat "Allah inflicts humiliation and scorn upon those who disobey."
2. In the beginning, the Arabian Peninsula (read utopia) has been set upon by locusts (crusader armies). All Muslims are victims and should, therefore, all agree upon a course of action.
3. One geographical area, the U.S., and another historical period, the middle ages an a metaphysical belief, paganism, are grouped together in the "them" category and another geographical area comprised of several countries and Muslims and victims are categorized under the "us" category.
4. The Americans have occupied Iraq, using the Peninsula as a staging post even though its rulers are against it.
5. Zionists are now added to the "them" category and a motivation (attempting to repeat massacres) is assigned to "them."
6. The motivation is made more personal: "They come to annihilate and humiliate."
7. Countries are categorized by assigning broad religious convictions to their citizens and attributing religious and economic motivations to one category: the "them" category.
8. All of the proceeding actions by Americans are a "clear declaration of war on Allah" and an imperative to action is introduced: Jihad is an individual duty if the enemy destroys Muslim countries.
9. On the basis of the proceeding claims, and with reference to a specific reading of a religious text, and "in compliance with Allah's order," the following fatwa is issued.
10. Fatwa: Kill Americans and their allies both civilian and military.
11. Take this action with reference to God and to free the oppressed. Note the implicit assumption that killing Americans

and their allies will achieve this goal without any account of
the potential negative, or even contrary, results.

12. Satan is added to the "them" category and "every Muslim"
    under the "us" category: "We call on every Muslim in all
    walks of life to launch the raid on Satan's U.S. troops and the
    devil's supporters allying with them." So now the categories
    look like this: "Them": Americans, Zionists, Crusaders, pa-
    gans, Satan. "Us": Arabian Peninsula, all Muslims, victims.

13. Another reference to religious text is cited.

14. A threat is directed at the audience: The next world is prefer-
    able to this one and "unless you go forth He will punish you
    with grievous penalty."

15. The audience is urged not to despair about its assigned vic-
    tim status, but rather, "to be true in faith and gain Mastery."

## LOGICAL FALLACIES

- The initial and most obvious problems with the logical structure
  of both narratives is that they begin with *unverifiable premises.*
  Begging the Questions means basing a conclusion on a premise
  that is in as much need of proof as the conclusion itself. We can't
  get to the conclusion if we doubt the veracity of the premises, for
  example: "Americans are once again trying to repeat the horrific
  massacres," or, "The problem with humanity is not so much one
  of ideology…but rather one of blood," or "If Blacks and Mexicans become a majority, then they will not be able to maintain
  the White man's social, cultural and economic systems because
  they do not have minds needed to do so…"

- Unverifiable premises often involve *universal claims of agreement.* Universal statements rarely have a place in credible narratives but claims of universal agreement are even more dubious,
  for example, "…all people of the Peninsula have acknowl-

edged…" or "No one argues three facts that are known to every-one."

- Tu Quoque Fallacy (familiar to any parent) is an argument that because someone else has done something first, there is nothing wrong with doing it second. The illogic of that claim goes something like this: Warring parties have often victimized civilians. Therefore: We can victimize civilians. But of course it is plausible to think that victimizing civilians is immoral in both instances.

Faulty analogy suggests that two things are more similar than they really are, "Blacks and Mexicans" conflates skin color with race and race and skin color with national identity. National identity is confused with religious identity, and civilians are alienated with aggressors on one side but not the other.

- Non-sequiturs are arguments in which the conclusion does not follow from the premise, for example, if you are a Muslim you will kill pagans.
- Bifurcation Fallacy is committed when a false dilemma is presented, for example, when the audience is asked to choose between two options when more options are available. The Jihad text would have the audience believe that if one is a Muslim one must either kill infidels or be punished. The Stormfront text would have the audience believe that if one is white one is either committed to "White Nationalism" or one is delusional, cowardly, and treacherous.

Ultimately, these narrators are not asking for agreement nor are these narratives dialogic; they are not to be understood as invitations for the target audience to share their opinions on the matters raised. These narratives are examples of appeals to consequence. The appeal to consequences is not an argument; it is a threat veiled as an argument. Just because non-belief or non-action in accordance with a fatwa may be met with punishment, for example, is not evidence that the action or the belief itself is justified.

Anyone who is inclined to be unsympathetic with these texts can immediately see the multiple and overlapping logical inconsistencies: affirming the consequent, arguments from ignorance, circular reasoning, moral equivalency, appeals to consequence, to name a few. An unsympathetic audience will also notice that these narratives have more in common than one might have initially expected, in fact, they are remarkably similar in both structure and content. Both narrators present themselves and those like them as "victims" of "others." Both are fear-based narratives. They both have a familiar structure. Both have idealized beginnings but there is no specific reference to where or when that time was. This is particularly true of the Stormfront text. The Jihad text presumably locates the time in the pre-crusade Arabian Peninsula. They both have a conflicted middle and locate the present in the middle of the narrative. Both narratives project a future which can either be a return to the utopian beginning or a disastrous end depending upon the audiences actions.

These narratives have a pretense of logical argument but the fact that they are illogical is irrelevant to their persuasive power for those who are vulnerable.

## WHITE SPACE EXCEPTIONS TO THE DOMINANT NARRATIVES THAT ARE SILENCED BY THE TEXT

In the second part of this chapter I am looking, in the Derridian fashion, for narrative material that is silenced by the text. I am not imposing narrative material from outside the narratives conceptual scheme but rather looking for what the strategically constructed world-view of the narrator omits. In order to re-structure alternative narratives it is imperative to access information that is contrary to the pathologizing narrative. That doesn't mean we make up information, it means that we go in search of it within the text itself.

The following list of information silenced by the terrorist texts makes no pretense to being exhaustive; the reader may contribute to it.

- Both texts allow only one of two ways for the audience to identify themselves. The Jihad text would have us think that there are two types of Muslims: victims and avengers. The vast majority of Muslims who are neither of these are silenced. The Stormfront text explicitly states that the audience either submits to the authority of the text or are otherwise traitors, cowards, or mentally unstable.
- Both narratives begin by assuming that the clear and distinct racial divisions are a fact, a reality, and then go on to represent racial segregation as a natural state and represent diverse populations living together as unnatural.
- Alternatively, category distinctions are blurred when, for example, the Jihad text conflates Islam (the faith) with Islamism (the political ideological tool) thereby creating the false impression that a shared religious identity entails a shared political agenda, a distinction that Quilliam, a Muslim anti-terror think tank, wants to make very clear, "The issue is not one of political correctness; it is about avoiding inaccuracies which unwittingly endorse and strengthen extremist narratives....The first step toward doing so is to avoid echoing Islamist language" (p. 2).
- Both narrators represent Caucasians as Christians. Obvious evidence to the contrary is not included in these representations as contrary evidence would disrupt the world-view the narrators are attempting to establish.
- Dissent within communities is silenced with phrases like "no one argues" and "unanimously agree." The texts would have their respective audiences assume, along with them, that if one is

Muslim, one identifies with this narrative and if one is categorized as Caucasian one agrees with the other.
- Ignoring the internal diversity and marginalizing religious mi-
  norities in large non-Muslim populations in countries like Egypt,
  Syria, and Pakistan silences them.
- The Jihad narrative excludes the fact that the Saudi government
  has, for its own self-interest, allowed American military bases in
  the land of Mecca.
- The Jihad text silences the casualty count resultant of the in-
  fighting between Sunies and Shea's.
- The text silences the role of Muslim dictators who have massa-
  cred Muslim citizens in their own countries.
- The equation of Americans with Christians and Arabs with Islam
  omits all the Americans who are not Christians and people who
  live in the Arabian Peninsula who are not Muslim.
- The text privileges the interpretation of the Koran by some Muslims over others thereby silencing the others.
- It silences Muslim victims of Muslim violence including women,
  children, civilians, and pilgrims. These victims are silenced but
  they still belong to this narrative, even by omission.
- Muslims must identify themselves as victims of Western aggression if the call to violent action is to be heeded. All instances of
  cooperation and alliance are omitted as they do not contribute to
  the conflict narrative.
- The Stormfront text silences all those whose vote is not determined by skin color.
- It silences Caucasians who are neither victims nor disillusioned
  or crazy.
- It silences the contributions of "Blacks and Mexicans."

Embedded in the narrative are discernable rules for the selection
of information. Both narratives in question begin with paradise
(past), move to paradise lost (present), then foresee paradise re-
gained (future). All the other events that don't fit neatly into this

narrative structure are omitted. To include that which has been excluded would be to interrupt the linear trajectory thereby loosening the grip of the conflict saturated narrative.

## NARRATIVE CONTRABAND: FROM DESCRIPTION TO PRESCRIPTION

In the last section I gave voice to information that is contrary to the terrorist texts and is therefore left out of the terrorism narratives trajectory. Now let us look at what the texts import under the radar. When we narrate we are not engaged in a neutral activity. And there is a collection of culturally available canonical forms that are considered appropriate for the expression of experience. These canonical forms mediate experience and normalize themselves. What seems like description is not, it is normalized, becomes canonical, and then that description becomes prescription.

When the dominant discourse has taken authority it has the power to enlist not only the cooperation but the collaboration of the audience in their own oppression. I am not suggesting the vulnerable targets of these narratives will intentionally omit facts contrary to the theme; they will simply be blind to them while simultaneously being pre-disposed to select instances that support the theme.

The genius of both narratives is getting the listener first to identify with victim status and then to blame himself for the future victimization of other people ("his" people) unless he takes violent action. If the audience can separate themselves from the problem or "externalize" the problem as Michael White has said, then it becomes possible to see events or experiences in a way in which the person is not the problem. And once the notion of a "true" narrative is called into question and the normalizing function of narrative is brought out into light, individuals may feel less compelled to live as supporting characters in narratives told at their expense.

The normalizing effects of a powerful narrative represent the political, economic, and ego interests of power, and those in power, as just the way things are, as natural, and as some sort of metaphysical reality. Recall that the narrator of the Stormfront text says "I am a lover of truth— that which is independent of the beliefs and attitudes of the observer." And he explicitly states that the truth he is telling is independent of the beliefs and attitudes of the narrator himself. In other words he is claiming to be a neutral observer witnessing some sort of natural phenomena, sort of like saying that if a tree falls in the forest it makes a sound even if there is no one there to hear it but this narrator is there to hear it. While "truth" may be independent of the beliefs and attitudes of the observer, the "observation" of it is not. Narratives are not like trees. And the category confusion is not accidental. Narrative is by its nature strategic. It is a rendering of events and actions and characters in a certain way for a certain purpose. The purpose is persuasion. The method is identification or as I prefer, mis-identification. Representing motivated world-views as naturally occurring metaphysical realities is a manipulative rhetorical move; it is strategic. It works even better if the narrator can get the audience to personalize political/economic/metaphysical conflicts. That is a good persuasive move, if it works, and it has. The obvious counter claim is that phenomena like geo/political conflicts are not neutral or disinterested.

Canonical styles of expression conspire to create a false impression that ideas and interests and motivation are fixed metaphysical realities. And if the narrator can blur the line between internal and external, between personal and group identity, between descriptions and prescriptions; then the normalizing power of narrative has taken hold. That is how ideologies are accorded truth status.

# THE WAR ON TERROR:
## "THEIR" NARRATIVE AND "OURS"

The United States, following the events of 9/11, and certain terrorist organizations have something in common according to psychiatrist Vamik Volkan; both groups show signs and symptoms of large group regression resulting from the experience of massive trauma. That trauma is an assault on group identity that results in a "shared attempt to protect, maintain, or repair the large-group identity and separate it from the 'enemy's identity." Volkan's metaphor for group identity is a tent that houses individuals. In normal non-regressed conditions the individuals living under the tent are not particularly concerned with the canvas or the poles holding up the tent. They are, rather, concerned with their own lives, their careers, their children. But under regressed conditions those personal considerations take a back seat and holding up the tent becomes the overwhelming preoccupation. The *method* of holding up the tent is what concerns us here. Volkan's claim is that trauma to group identity leads to group regression which in turn lends itself to a shared attempt to "protect, maintain, or repair the large-group identity and separate it from the 'enemies' identity" (2). He defines regression in groups the same way it is defined in individuals— as a mental defense mechanism which involves regression to an earlier stage of human development that results from stress, trauma, and threat. He stresses that regression is neither good nor bad but an inevitable by-product of trauma and demonstrates that the post 9/11 American identity shares characteristic behaviors with other groups whose identity has been threatened. Some of those behaviors include: an emotional sensitivity to national borders, an increased reliance on "us" and "them" attitude, rigidified morality, conflating religion and politics, the use of proto-symbols, splitting of perceptions black/white and good/bad without recognition of gray areas, and the continual reactivation of shared triumphs and traumas that have become markers of the group's identity,

Introjection (what I have been calling internalization) and pro-
jection are, according to Volkin, psychic defense mechanisms regressed populations tend to use. While well-balanced individuals
may internalize and project to some degree, regressed individuals
use them extensively and unconsciously. The same is true for
groups,

> increased collective introjection results in very strictly incorpo-
> rating new political or religious ideas or doctrines, as if the very
> identity of the regressed large group fed on such ideas and doc-
> trines to keep itself alive. Shared projection, on the other hand,
> magnifies the present dangers posed by "others"...a regressed
> group becomes involved in more activities that maintain the
> *'existence' (identity)* of the group (Volkin, 2012, p. 3).

Those sorts of activities may involve aggression toward others,
survival behavior, and a group idealization of victimization. Recall
in the "Jihad" text, for example, the emphasis on victimization
(humiliation, terrorizing, wiping out, plundering, dictating) and in
the "Stormfront" text the emphasis on victimization is similar (the
grave situation, unfairness).

As we have seen in terrorist texts, "regressed large groups also
exhibit severe splitting...Perceptions become 'black and white,'
'good and bad' with no allowance for 'gray' areas. Recall the
Stormfront text creates dichotomies like "good" and "bad" people
and creates arbitrary separations of geographical regions like Iraq,
Somalia, and Mexico on one side and the United States and Europe
on the other. Then there is the categorizing, as confused as it is, of
"Blacks," "Mexicans," and "Browns" on one side and "Whites" on
the other. And the "Jihad" text separates Muslims on one side and
Americans on the other thereby blurring the clear distinction between religion and nationality and between sects in Islam and between civilians and military, and simultaneously creating an arbitrary distinction between Muslims, people who live in the Arabian

Peninsula, victims, on the one hand, and Americans, Pagans, Crusaders on the other.

Note also that in traumatized regressed groups, spatial borders and tangible distinctions assume a new intensity, "Related to the concern with psycho-spatial borders is the preoccupation with 'blood,' contamination, and group homogeneity…Of the group regression is malignant, this preoccupation may lead to the worst human horrors: ethnic cleansing, even genocide" (p. 5).

Volkan describes the role of large group trauma in creating an atmosphere that supports terrorist attacks.

> …although the actual event may be centuries old, the mental representation of it is embedded in the group's sense of identity and may, when reactivated, provide fuel for aggression or a sense of victimhood in the present day. Many leaders know how to stimulate chosen traumas and glories a well as how to bring to bear on present issues the emotions pertaining to those past events, thus magnifying both fears and defenses against such fears (4).

This is the sort of trauma, resulting from the events of 9/11 and the "war on terror" narrative used to frame the experience, that futurist and middle-east expert Amy Zalman warns should not be allowed to weave itself into American identity, "by assigning it an iconographic status on par with national myths of manifest destiny and the frontier nation.…A principle reason for the durability of the global war on terror is that it represents an extraordinarily powerful narrative, which Obama will need to re-write." (Zalman, 2).

Signs that a traumatized group is moving out of regression into being a "progressed" group are characterized by:

1. Valuing freedom of speech and just functioning of existing civic institutions.
2. Raising new generations of children with intact "basic trust" and maintaining existing family structures.

3. Halting the devaluation of women.
4. Re-establishing family and clan ties as more important than ties to political or religious ideologies and the personality of the leader.
5. Separating fantasy from reality and past from present.
6. Preserving individuality, the capacity for compromise, and the ability to question what is moral or beautiful.

*Chapter Four*

# Psychological Warfare

*Colonizing Narratives as Recruitment Strategy*

## INTRODUCTION

There is general agreement among national security specialists that dealing effectively with terrorism is going to require going beyond traditional strategies of warfare not only because terrorists' tactics exceed those of traditional warfare but also because of what is being fought over. This is an ideological struggle in which military might is ineffectual. Drones cannot "neutralize" ideas. We have to out-think the opponent. The battleground is the philosophical arena. As the 9/11 Commission concluded, prevailing over *ideology* is required to eliminate terrorist threat (9/11 Commission Report, 2004. p. 363). Indeed as Brian Michael Jenkins of RAND has clarified,

> American is not "at war" with terrorism. Terrorism is a phenomenon, not a foe…It is not sufficient to merely outgun the terrorists. The enemy here is more than just a group, it is an ideology, a set of attitudes, a belief system organized into a recruiting network that will replace terrorist losses unless ultimately defeated politically (Sept. 8, 2002).

35

Despite this widely acknowledged state of affairs there is under-
standable public discomfort about engaging in a blatantly ideological struggle particularly one that is not above-board like a philosophical debate would be. Talk of the psychological aspects of
ideological transformation have therefore been euphemistically referred to as "political warfare" (Jenkins, June 26, 2005) or as "strategic influence" (Gough, April 7, 2004). The term "Psychological
Warfare" makes us uncomfortable because the term is associated
with psychological manipulation, disinformation campaigns, propaganda, brain-washing and mind control.

Despite these discomforts, long before the events of 9/11, we
were already engaged, even by default, in psychological warfare,
call it what you will, that has already involved all of the unpleasant-
ly associated tactics just listed. And it isn't just used by what is
commonly thought of as one side of a conflict against the other.
Terrorist recruiters also use psychological warfare against the individuals they recruit and that is the subject of this chapter.

The technique in question has been implemented by imperial
powers over entire populations and the effects are much more insidious than the effects of physical force and last long after the
initial psychological assault because the power of this technique
lies in getting the audience to oppress itself. The technique to which
I refer is the implementation of a colonial Master narrative as a
method of psychological warfare. A colonizing narrative is one that
appears to be a neutral description of a state of affairs but is, in fact,
ideologically empowered, strategically implemented, and motivated to control behavior.

In this chapter I am focusing on the way in which linguistic and
discursive traditions, specifically in the form of colonizing narratives, work to ascribe identity in the interest of getting individuals
to regulate themselves. What I am undertaking is an examination of
the mechanisms and effects of ideological legitimization. My *question* is, how do ideologically driven world-views get accorded truth

status thereby appearing to be natural rather than constructed, neutral rather than motivated, and obvious rather than questionable? My *approach* is deconstructive similar to the way feminists deconstruct patriarchal legitimacy, and post-modernists uncover the methods through which power regulates knowledge. My *goal* is to destabilize the insidious psychological effects of colonizing narrative by exposing its techniques.

## INTERNALIZATION

The French historian Michel Foucault uncovered techniques and practices far more effective and longer lasting than physical force to alter and control individuals - techniques that get people to internalize the interests of external powers. These are techniques that recruit individuals to play an active part in their own oppression so that an authoritarian ideology is internalized and continued by the individual. In contrast, the behavioral effects of torture will only last as long as it, or the fear of it, lasts. And physical coercion will not cause an ideological shift and may even have the opposite effect. If, on the other hand, an individual can be encouraged to internalize external authority there is no need for continued external force. The force will come from within, "each individual under its weight will end by interiorizing to the point that he is his own overseer, each individual thus exercising this surveillance over, and against, himself."

Foucault's list of regulatory techniques includes classifications, isolation, intimidation, surveillance, and ascriptions of identity, all elements of colonizing narratives. Colonizing narratives implement those strategies all by storytelling, and telling again, and again. The continued repetition is essential and is carried out and continued by the audience.

Foucault performed what he called "archaeologies" of institutional powers that are responsible for constructing what is generally thought of as a person's identity, a person's values, beliefs, and behavior. He demonstrated that socially instituted and maintained norms within a particular culture rely on the repetition of identity practices, for example, gendered norms are constructed by the repetition of behaviors (passivity, physical weakness, emotionality, or alternatively, aggression, dominance, rationality) that are generally considered *results* of or *expressions* of, those gendered norms. So, for example, there was a time when women were thought to be "hysterical" by nature. It is now understood that what was described as hysteria became a social norm that was "ascribed" or attributed to women who, in turn, took on/in the description as a prescription and acted hysterically and in so doing encouraged hysterical behaviors in other women and so on. Hysteria became "normalized" and idealized by the repeated practices of it. These sorts of mimetic practices, according to Foucault, maintain and then reproduce, regulate, repeat, and thereby legitimate what become norms. That process, of creating the "normal" out of motivated ideologies (often referred to as "normalizing" or "normative operations") is not in the self-interest of those who continue the process.

Normative constructions and practices, along with their coercive and limiting consequences, can be de-stabilized by exposing and advertising their regulatory functions. In the interest of de-stabilizing colonizing terrorist recruitment narratives and the ideologies that inform them, let us first look at what colonizing narratives are and how they operate.

## DEFINITION AND FEATURES
## OF COLONIZING NARRATIVES

Founding members of the field of inquiry referred to as colonial discourse theory are Edward Said, (*Orientalism,* 1978), Homi Bhabha, (*The Location of Culture*, 1994) and Gayatri Spivak, (*In Other Worlds: Essays in Cultural Politics*, 1987). They initiated a systematic examination of the ways colonial discourse operates as an instrument of power. A definition of colonial discourse can be distilled from the work of these three theorists as linguistic practices deployed to manage colonizer's relationships with those they colonize. While it is generated by colonizers, through repetition, it becomes the discourse through which the colonized view themselves. It becomes internalized by the colonized. It is a form of control through rhetoric, "Imperial relations may have been established initially by guns, guile, and disease...but they were maintained...largely by textuality...colonialism...is an operation of discourse..." (Tiffin and Lawson, 1994).

My own definition of colonizing recruitment narratives includes the elements listed above *put into proto-typical form.* So this new definition involves four essential features: *structure, description, identity*, and *prescription*. First, the colonizing Master narrative organizes past events sequentially thereby (seemingly) showing (by implying) causality. The common yet erroneous cognitive connection between succession and cause/effect outlined in the first chapter goes by undetected. Examples of terrorist recruitment narratives that shared this structure were provided in the previous chapter. The familiar form of the story is described in a linear/unified/sequential fashion with an idealized utopian beginning, a conflicted current (middle) situation that encourages the audience to situate themselves (identify) with the good guys as victims, and concludes by compelling the audience to take action consistent with the projected future. This is done by alternately including and excluding information, assigning moral responsibility, cause and effect, and other narrative components to suit the agenda.

This type of narrative has been referred to by post-colonial theorists as Eurocentric, that is, it is attributed to British and European imperialist ideology motivated by interests in political/social/economic control over its subjects. Interestingly, if Brian Jenkins is right, and I think he is, that Islamist terrorists think strategically but not linearly or sequentially, (Jenkins, March 2, 2006), then it is possible that they have coopted a narrative form that lends itself to deception. Clearly recruitment narratives are linear and sequential in structure. Why do Islamist terrorists think one way and narrate another? The nature of colonization phenomena makes it impossible to know whether this coopting is intentional or if recruiters themselves have been colonized to the extent that they have internalized the Master narrative, subjugated themselves to it, and then uncritically keep repeating it, never suspecting that it is not their story.

The second feature, description, as we have seen in the previous chapter, often invokes analogies to things that are, in fact, not analogous (like skin pigmentation and national origin as in "Blacks and Mexicans," or the equation of Americans with pagans, or Arabs with Muslims) and simultaneously create artificial dichotomies (like ridged racial divisions).

The third and most insidious feature of colonizing narratives is enacted by the audience itself when it personally identifies with, internalizes, and takes responsibility for what has been described by the narrative's agenda as the ills of the social/political/historical/economic environment. This is psychological warfare at its most effective.

The fourth feature of colonizing narrative is prescription. When an individual is colonized he is re-described and re-defined such that the identity being described is the identity being created. Description becomes prescription, that is, the description is normalized, repeated, such that behaviors resulting from the original description were determined *by* it.

The contemporary rock star of colonial identity constructions and post-colonial responses, Gayatri Spivak, defines ideology, with uncharacteristic simplicity, as "an unquestioningly accepted system of ideas that takes material shape in social action" and connects ideology to the "politics of explanation" which encourage modes of behavior that produce and reproduce the same models of explanation and "take so little notice of the politico-economic-technological determinant" that they seem like an instrument of explanation rather than being constitutive of the thing being explained (1987, p. 108–111).

Let me be more explicit about the symbiotic nature of terrorism and colonialism. I am not just claiming that they are similar or that they are connected, but rather, that one is a variety of the other. They are both forms of psychological warfare and share all the same features.

Philip Taylor defines psychological warfare as "psychological activities in peace or war, directed at the enemy, friendly and neutral audiences, in order to influence attitudes and behavior affecting the achievement of political and military objectives" (1999). And Ashis Nandy shows us that the most dangerous and permanent effects of colonialism are psychological, "…the ultimate violence which colonialism does to its victims …it creates a culture in which the ruled are constantly tempted to fight their rulers within the psychological limits set by the later" (p. 3). But Nandy shows us much more than limits. He points to a cognitive superiority that should be maintained rather than thrown out in favor of Master discourse. According to Nandy, the slave represents a higher order cognition which includes the Master as human. This is contrary to Master cognition which views the slave as "thing," "Ultimately, modern oppression, as opposed to traditional oppression, is not an encounter between self and enemy…It is a battle between dehumanized self and the objectified enemy" (p. 16).

What Alex Schmid has observed about the evolution in thought about terrorist methods is equally true for the evolution in thought about colonial methods, "For too long terrorism has been understood primarily in terms of (political) violence. Gradually, it has been realized that it should be understood more in terms of communication or propaganda (2014, p. 1).

An essential feature of that propaganda is what Schmid thinks it imperative to counter, al Qaeda's single narrative, "The 'single' in 'single narrative' refers to the fact that al Qaeda has merged a number of historical grievances existing in the Arab and Muslim world into a consolidated body and attributed the causes for diverse woes that affect Islam to outside actors, namely, 'Crusaders and Jews' and local rulers allegedly serving their purposes" (2014, p. 5). I think this definition of single narrative is part of what Ashis Nandy refers to as colonizer's framework within which the oppressed assume are the limits of their ability to respond. Al Qaeda is not alone in assuming this framework, as I have pointed out; "we" share the assumption. It is a colonial assumption, a weak assumption, an unimaginative assumption. And yet, it is a very persuasive assumption, and does a lot of work, as long as it is not challenged. This book constitutes a challenge to that assumption.

The single narrative Schmid uncovers is a Master narrative in content and in form— a Master narrative that I have been arguing should be thrown off, destabilized, subverted, called out, and otherwise challenged, in favor of multiple narrative structures wherein competing and even incommensurate narratives can coexist without being synthesized and homogenized into a singular over-riding entity. Relatedly, as I argued in the first chapter, singular/unified structure treats time linearly, that is, there is an assumed progression that moves from beginning to middle to end. This inherited conceptual framework undervalues any element of history that is disjunctive. But it is there, in the space left by the disjunctive past that we find exceptions to the dominant singular party-line. It is in the cracks in continuity that we find the exceptions that can be elements of a new narrative. A new narrative can circumvent unilinear notions of progress and can take advantage of ideological distastes for disjunction. A new narrative form can traverse temporal sequential ordering by blurring the modern European cognitive separation between past, present, and future, for example, by reviving pre-colonized epic and mythological narrative forms and their attendant ontologies.

*Chapter Five*

# Post-Colonial Practices
# and Narrative Nomads

## INTRODUCTION

I begin by assuming three things. First, I assume that the institutions of colonization continue to function in a colonized culture even after the withdrawal of a physical colonial presence. Second, I assume a particular type of colonization phenomenon among indigenous elites which involves appropriating the Master Narrative. My third assumption is that human experience, cognition and identity are fundamentally narrative in nature. Having made similar assumptions, a number of theorists have focused on issues of cross-cultural conflict, physical dislocation and experiential rupture in the formation of subjectivity. Critical engagement with colonial narratives and the re-examination of indigenous pre-colonized narratives has been recently popular. Some have engaged in unlearning privilege, while others have examined the practical methods, and unique position, of subaltern subjects who have managed to maintain indigenous ways of being while simultaneously adapting to colonial impositions. Following this line of inquiry, I am interested in the possibility of the formulation of new narratives which make sense of (but do not necessarily integrate) one's cultural past with the subject effects of colonialism. I will suggest that rather than attempting to create a central space, the project should be to fully embody hybrid ontologies and to identify with dislocation. The project should be to fully occupy marginal space.

My initial concern is to disentangle the existential situations of immigrants from those of what I refer to as cultural nomads or multicultural subjects— the children or grandchildren of immigrants. Then I trace the colonial subject's initial linguistic dislocation, through epistemological and ontological displacement. And finally, I explore varieties of post-colonial agency that involve extricating oneself from inherited constraints and authorizing oneself in the margins between cultures. All this will be done from my standpoint as a member of the Sikh diaspora—a first-generation American with a hybrid ontology engaged in an effort to reverse the imperial gaze and to deconstruct the insidious mechanisms of colonization that continue to operate long after the withdrawal of a physical colonial presence.

The consequences of this endeavor are significant; I will demonstrate the way in which multicultural existence is a crucial exception to the "death of the subject" proclaimed by postmodernists (Barths 1977, Foucault 1977). It is an exception to the culturally determined nature of human existence proclaimed by contemporary philosophers and cognitive scientists (Johnson 1993, 5). And multiculturalism is a way out of the limitations placed on creativity and imagination by the conceptual schemes of one culture (Johnson 1993, 5; Lakoff and Johnson 1980; Quine 1951).

## TYPES OF DIASPORA:
## IMMIGRANTS AND CULTURAL NOMADS

Diasporic populations encounter unique challenges resulting from conflicting systems of identification, particularly if colonization is a part of the cultural history. But there is a distinction between being an immigrant and being part of the diaspora born in a land other than that from which one's parents or grandparents came, and that difference is most evident in the respective capacities to go beyond colonial designations and the preconceived identity categories of any one culture.

Immigrants once belonged to, and were formed in accordance with, a culturally specific conceptual apparatus. The immigrant has a home but does not live there, has a language not often spoken and has habits and modes of thought which are consistent with one culture's norms. While immigrants have imposed upon themselves a sort of exile from their traditions, histories and cultures, the children of immigrants are exiled from the very notion of an original language, exiled from any memory of a home-land, exiled from the very possibility of an identity consistent with one culture's norms. A multicultural subject, one who is familiar with more than one culture and more than one language, has access to multiple cultures/languages/conceptual systems but is not, like those comfortably enculturated, determined by them. A cultural nomad cannot call one language a mother tongue or one place a home. Concepts like homeland, mother tongue and nationalist identity are only inherited baggage for the nomad.

The distinction between the existential situations of immigrants and those of cultural nomads is a crucial one; failure to make the distinction results both in immigrants imposing their alienation upon future generations, and in multicultural subjects appropriating alienation that is not their own. I am suggesting that the sense of loss, deprivation and nostalgia that saturates the narratives of cultural nomads and linguistic border dwellers (Derrida 1998) is evidence of the appropriation of a false memory and then the development of artificial longing for what it rep- resents. A brief example, which involves the identity or identification of generations of Sikhs born outside Punjab, will clarify my perspective: The longing for the home- land is legitimate only for those who were born or lived in Punjab. For the rest of us, longing for a home we have never known, and then creating a connection between that imagined home and one's identity, is an example of appropriation of an older generation's alienation. It is the appropriation of an existential situation, and an accompanying mythology, that is not our own. This is but one example of the way in which those of us in the diaspora self-impose a sort of double-bind of not belonging where we belong and of yearning for a home we have never known. Rather than attempting to create a central space for ourselves, the project should be to more fully embody hybrid ontologies, and to identify with dislocation. The goal should be to fully occupy our marginal space.

The construction of fictional memory of an original culture from which one can mourn being exiled is a way to align one's cultural alienation with a recognizable form of alienation within a culture, but to do so is to misidentify. It is a form of self-deception. The nomad experiences something far more profound than simply being removed from original home/language/culture. The nomad is removed from the very possibility of such. For the nomad, these things have not been lost—there is nothing of them to remember. However, this sort of existential status is not lamentable, as it holds immense constructive possibilities.

The potential capacity for response to colonial impositions results from marginalization and displacement. As a minority community historically defined by exclusion and difference from the dominant discourses of Hinduism and Islam, Sikhs are in a uniquely subversive position. One of the ethical problems with thinking of Sikh identity as consistent and central is the resulting division of "others" as "same" or "different." If identity (in this case defined as "sameness" or idam) is not privileged over difference, then the basis for ethical action shifts. Our pre-colonized ontology defends pluralism and violates caste systems and gendered social roles. This historical positioning, combined with the transnational and multilinguistic nature of multiculturalism, enables access to multiple stories, voices and conceptual schemes. Existence between authoritarian discourses of dominant cultures enables an extended form of agency wherein one who exists between cultures can undermine traditional associations, assumptions and identity practices, while at the same time creating narrative connections between otherwise incommensurable world-views.

There are multiple potential problems associated with existence outside any one culture's norms. The problems have to do with a perceived inability to "ground" oneself and one's actions resulting from intimate familiarity with cultural relativism:

1. The difficulty of speaking in "one's own voice" or from a singular perspective voice when one has not one, but multiple voices resulting from experiences in a multitude of places and in various languages.
2. The problems with consistent identity associated with cultural dislocation, including being the object of radically inconsistent, even incommensurable, cultural norms.
3. The confusion resulting from colonial appropriations, and the reappropriations of colonized ontologies.
4. The conflict of hybrid ontologies.
5. The Western tradition of monolingualism and narrative unity require too much experiential negation on the part of multicultural subjects.

Let me address the fifth, and least self-explanatory, of these difficulties. While many contemporary theorists insist on the inadequacy of Western narrative structure for our "narrative identities," our own traditions don't provide accessible alternatives. The Eastern sense of self is completely bound up with ancestral site, with family, with social place. Radical dislocation, lack of ancestral figures with whom one can identify and the unashamed use and manipulation of language make the traditional sense of self inaccessible to many of us. The Western ego-ideals of singularity and autobiographical unity create the appearance of what has been described as inconsistent, fragmentary, discontinuous beings. The Western normative ideal for auto- biographical narrative—that is, linearity and unity—requires psychological repression even in Western subjects, but requires an even greater self-effacement on the part of multicultural subjects. The ideal of a unified self not only requires a brand of self-imposed amnesia, it also has the effect of marginalizing non-unified or discontinuous autobiographies as hysteric, random and incoherent. Cultural nomads are forced to look beyond either tradition, and yet neither tradition is left behind. This is what Spivak refers to as new narrations of older scripts (Landry and Maclean 1996, 27). History must not be denied; it must be imbued with various alternative meanings.

There is evidence (Kumar 1994) which suggests that the 'contextualization' practiced by Eastern colonial subjects causes less cognitive dissonance than it would for Western subjects. Contextualization is a particularly effective adaptive strategy for dealing with colonial cultural impositions. It involves the cognitive separation of activities in which physical separation is symbolic of cultural difference. For example, Western influence in the East has created a rift between the place/ space where one works and the space/place where one lives. So in adapting, or contextualizing, someone might dress for work in Western-style garments and speak English, while at home revert back to traditional ways of life without any conflict.

These compartmentalized ways of being are at odds with Western consciousness, which aims at universalistic principles of behavior and could potentially cause considerable cognitive dissonance in a Western subject. The Western assumption of the ego-ideal of self and identity that is orientated towards integration and consistency is problematic in situations in which there are conflicting social roles, commitments, interests, duties and so forth. Eastern subjects have inherited a self-structure that is contextualized and highly relational so that inconsistency is not a threat to oneself.

While this sort of identity-dependent-on-cultural-context may seem like multiple personality disorder as there is no unifying Grand Narrative presiding over the collection of culturally specific narratives, there is an associative self-structure based on place/space and memory rather than on temporally linear narrative constructions. Embodied memory is the central axis.

## THE HERMENEUTICS OF COLONIZATION AND REVERSING THE GAZE

The cycles of colonization, translation, appropriation, mastery and recognition form a hermeneutic circle involving varieties of literal colonization of one culture by another and various levels of appropriation of the colonizer's ontologies by the colonized.

The first tier of the interpretative cycle has at least three distinct phases enacted by the colonizer and three phases enacted by the colonized. The colonizer engages in linguistic translation of "native" language and usage, cultural translation in an attempt to make 'native' culture comprehensible and translation of the subject, which involves a literal alteration in the ontology of the subject resulting from linguistic and cultural translation. Then, enacted by the colonially altered subject, are the processes of appropriation of the master language/culture/identity, recognition of oneself as other through the master's gaze and alienation resulting from loss of one's original language/culture/identity and from the inability to return to a pre-colonized ontology. The following section is an archaeology of the colonial practice of ultimate translation: translation of the subject.

## Translation: Linguistic, Cultural, Subjective

Translation, beginning with linguistic translation, is an appropria-
tive act. Translation in colonial/imperialistic contexts alters the
thing being translated. When a culture has been colonized, it is re-
described and re-defined in colonial terms such that while the colonizer may consciously be attempting to describe the language/cul-
ture/subject, he or she is actually creating the language/culture/
subject he/she thinks is being described. For example, the production of textual translations, dictionaries and grammar books by the
British in India converted Indian languages (Persian, Sanskrit, Pun-
jabi, Urdu and Hindi) into instruments of colonial rule. The lack of
correspondence between Indian and British linguistic, conceptual
and even metaphysical systems was compensated for in translation.
Discursive formations established correspondences, artificial correspondences, that would make the unfamiliar comprehensible. For
example, Brahman was translated as "priest" (Cohn 1996, 19). That
sort of translation had the effect of diminishing an entire range of
ways of being and simultaneously marginalizing the subject.

In British translations, meaning was attributed to a word, a sentence or a phrase. And meaning could be determined and translated
through a supposed synonym. It was also assumed that the meaning
of a word, sentence or phrase had a direct referent. But meaning is
determined and understood differently by an Indian subject, for
whom there may or may not be a direct referent. For example, to try
to infer the meaning of nam simran by attempting to determine
what it refers to is to misunderstand. Its referent is over-deter-
mined. While nam refers to the nam and simran is a verb denoting a
repetitive practice, the meaning, if it can be understood that way at
all, has to do with the effect on one's state of being.

Another example of linguistic/cultural/subjective translation is
the way in which lines of kinship were translated by the British. In
Indian cultures, one refers to one's sibling and one's cousin with
the same word. There is no distinction, linguistic or otherwise,

between one's sibling and one's cousin. Alternatively, there are several different words and relationships for the English concept "uncle." In an Indian context, there is a distinction made between an uncle on the maternal side and an uncle on the paternal side. Still further, there is a linguistic and correlative relational distinction between an uncle who is younger than one's parent and an uncle who is older than one's parent. So there is one designation for Mother's younger brother, another designation for Mother's older brother, another for Father's older brother and yet another designation for Father's younger brother. There is also a different designation for maternal and paternal grandparents. All these differences are translated into English by diminishing those sorts of subtleties.

The linguistic distinctions in these kinship lines are not just linguistic; they refer to distinctions in kinship patterns. They refer to patterns of behavior, to roles and responsibilities, to inheritances, to expectations and obligations. Those distinctions in kinship imply one person's ability to choose his own career and another's obligation to manage the family farm or business. They imply responsibilities for parental care-taking and ritual and ceremonial duties.

To diminish those linguistic differences in translation is to go well beyond linguistic translation; it is an example of cultural translation. Beyond that, it is an example of translating the subject. Within the colonial context, one can be no more than an "uncle." What happens to various roles and responsibilities? What happens to all the subtleties in ways of being and in relationships between family members? They are, of course, silenced, homogenized under the simplistic English category: "uncle."

Language is a part of a larger system of meaning, and those meanings are the results of cultural premises that may not be shared cross-culturally. Another example will further illustrate the incompatible cultural premises that evidence the problematic nature of translation: When written communication was received by British colonials, they would attempt to understand the meaning by translating the content of the letter. But for an Indian subject, the meaning of the communication would exceed the content of the message. As meaningful as, or even more meaningful than, the content of the message itself were, for example, the preliminary form of address, the material (parchment or fabric) the message was written on, the type of script used, the status of the messenger, the conveyance used to deliver the message, the manner in which the message was presented, and so forth (Cohn 1996, 19).

These observations lead to more essential questions about the nature of cross- cultural translation: Is translation, by nature, an act of appropriation? Is translation necessarily masterful or colonizing? Is it possible to translate while leaving the subject of translation intact?

It seems to me that translation is always, at least, mistaken if it places the text (and here I refer not only to a literal "text" but to "text" in the postmodern sense) in a certain and particular position and then ascertains "the" meaning or finds "the truth" "in" it. That sort of textual violence, of interpretation handed down from a presupposed position, renders the text voiceless. The text becomes subservient to one's assumptions if there is a pre-existent normative ideal and the non-conforming elements are silenced, repressed, marginalized, misread or misinterpreted.

When normative ideals precede textual exegesis the interpretation takes on a life of its own, cut off from one culture's traditions in service to another culture's assumptions. This phenomenon is particularly brutal in colonial contexts.

The Western insistence on the concrete as the stuff of knowledge has had its con- sequences. The colonial insistence on the effable, the translatable, on stable meaning, has rendered entire cultures mute. British translations never got beyond notions of meaning as fixed and stable across varying contexts or beyond clarity and distinctness in the Cartesian sense. The British search for meaning that was stable and could be categorized was an imperialist act. It is imperialist because in Indian contexts, statements, utterances, observations, stories, myths or kathas are not unconditional statements of fact but rather are highly provisional and contextualized. One gets closest to "the" meaning when one understands meaning as non-final and as codependent. So that while colonial translators thought of themselves as providing a framework within which meaning could be grasped, they were actually functioning to shape meaning in accordance with their own presupposed framework.

Acts of translation transpose something into something else. In colonial contexts this mutation becomes institutionalized. If there are no shared cultural premises, translation changes language such that the colonizer's culture becomes the privileged referent.

That is the insidious nature of colonization. That is the machinery through which it continues to operate long after the withdrawal of a physical colonial presence.

## Appropriating Memory

A second tier of the hermeneutic circle, enacted by second-generation immigrants or cultural nomads, may appear to repeat several phases of the previous generation, but there are significant shifts. The most significant among the shifts is that these interpretative processes are enacted internally rather than being imposed externally. Another significant shift is that these second-tier phases include not simple appropriation but the mastery of colonial language and the mastery of colonial cultural norms. There is a third aspect of second-generation diaspora that is of particular interest— the appropriation of the existential situation of the exile. This practice is what I refer to as an "autobiographical lie."

The mourning for the native culture is possible only for first-generation cultural exiles. The lie involves not only appropriating a masterful view of the "native's" predicament but also the appropriation of the older generation's alienation. In this sense, the second generation colonized is in a double-bind that is, in fact, self-imposed.

As a first-generation exile one can experience alienation of this sort, but for those of us in the diaspora this alienation is not our own. This is our parents' alienation and it is comparatively simplistic in form.

## Reversing the Gaze

A third level of the hermeneutic process includes: the deconstruction of colonial ontologies through an archaeology of that ontology that finds its roots as far back as linguistic interpretation of the colonized by the colonizer (as seen in the example of the translation into "uncle"); the recognition that even the master is a social construct and that master power is generated by the subjugated (an example of this phenomenon is the rejection of the practices of caste/class/racial/gender distinctions that are the complete antithesis of pre-colonized Sikh ontology); and, finally, the development of narrative authority without return to the myth of the original.

Having argued elsewhere (Maan 1999) against modernist notions of unified linear selfhood, and having argued in favor of understanding multicultural identity as highly contextualized, I want to add an essential cautionary note. There is a danger in multicultural existence; the danger is a sort of cultural relativism (and its consequences) that can result from being rooted in cultures with variant ontologies. The consequences of culturally relative identity constructions can be a sort of apathetic or even irresponsible stance— choosing not to ground authority in oneself or selves.

The problem is that shifts in narrative authority constitute a shift in the ground for ethical action. And having access to multiple cultural traditions can provide multiple ways out of taking an ethical stance or, alternatively, an ethical stance can subvert, embody and/or contribute to multiple cultural traditions. When theory and practice split, ethical action based on grounded narrative authority can remind a culture of its theory and traditions.

Taking narrative authority, self-authorship is a post-colonial practice. The action of choosing where to place 'one's' authority is central to understanding identity in any kind of personal sense. I use the term "self-authorship" to imply an interest in the self-creation of modernism mediated by a recognition of the involuntary aspects of existence of postmodernism. Self-authorship assumes a narrative nature of human experience but goes further than the narrative-identity theories of MacIntyre (1981) or Ricoeur (1983, 1985, 1988, 1991, 1992). Self-authorship is a variant of self-creation but the former integrates the postmodern critique of "selfhood" and therefore treats individual choice as limited to either acceptance of, reaction against or mediation of the involuntary aspects of existence. Self-authorship assumes that while a person comfortably grounded in one culture cannot get past its conceptual schemes (Quine 1951), one can mediate them creatively or, as Mark Johnson would caution, metaphorically (Johnson 1993). However, the mediation of conceptual schemes of various cultures enlarges one's existential choice. Multiculturalism provides this crucial exception to the otherwise determined nature of existence. Let me explain.

In light of the postmodern deconstruction of the modern "self," questions about what personal identity is, who has it, and how one becomes identified have been addressed by reference to various theories of social construction. A person is not, postmodernists claim, a freely choosing rational individual. In fact, the notions of free will and rationality are toppled, along with the possibility of individuality, by an archaeology of institutional powers that are responsible for constructing what had previously been thought of as a person, a person's identity, a person's body, a person's values, convictions, beliefs, behavior. Of these formative institutional powers, linguistic and discursive traditions are of particular interest to

those concerned with the possibilities for selfhood in an autobiographical sense.

Mediating the voluntary and the involuntary, the given and the
chosen, is a post- colonial attempt to move away from mimetic
identity practices toward some form of performative selves representation. Mimetic identity practices are those regulatory practices
that constitute the internal coherence of the subject, the self-identi-
cal status of a person. These are socially instituted and maintained
norms for intelligibility of 'personal' identity within a particular
culture. Mimetic identity practices create, maintain, reproduce, regulate and legitimize conformity. For example, gender categories are
constructed by the repetitive practices (passivity, sentimentality,
physical weakness or, alternatively, aggression, dominance, rationality) that are generally considered results of, or expressions of,
these very categories. And this type of repetitive performance not
only constructs but also regulates other performances.

At the other end of the spectrum are possibilities for self-creation consistent with the modernist notion of rugged individualism.
This extreme assumes, too optimistically, that individuals can liber-
ate themselves from normative conventions of identification and
create a self and a life by choosing. Existentialism is an example of
modern movements of self-creation.

Mediating the extremes of social construction and self-creation
is selves representation, which begins deconstructively by exposing
the coercive and limiting consequences of identity categories and
practices, and then destabilizes identity constructions by exposing
their normative regulatory functions. Selves representational identity is formed in the process of performing the identity that it is
purported to be.

The notion of self-authorship assumes a type of Internarrative
Identity (Maan 1999) created through the continual mediation of
pre-existent faulty conceptual separations of consciousness and
corporeality, individual and communal senses of self, self-creation

and social construction and singular unified self and multiple fractured personalities. The next section outlines a few of the preexistent faulty conceptual separations that the nomad must mediate and suggests forms that mediation might take.

## CONCEPTION OF THE SELF: EAST AND WEST

In Western traditions personal identity is based upon uniqueness and formed by separation. It has been observed that individuation seems to be the most crucial aspect of the Western autobiographical endeavor (Olney 1980, introduction). The hero of the traditional narrative is defined by exclusionary means, by distinction from the crowd. The heroes of the Western myth consider themselves and their opinions as the center of their own self-possession. Identity for them is intimately personal.

Alternatively, there is the possibility of identification through relationship rather than individuation. In Eastern traditions identity is understood as the identity of like things (the Sanskrit idam). This is shared sameness, sameness with others. The identity of the communal subject is completely contextualized and is consistent with, and embedded in, the space, place and culture in which it exists. Feminists have drawn our attention to the fact that women have long been identified primarily through their relationship with others. In Eastern contexts identity has to do with commonality rather than uniqueness. There is identification through relationship rather than individuation. The Eastern subject is a communal subject such that familial relations, hereditary place and ancestral ties are extremely important to identity formation. As one contemporary Indian poet put it, "I was taught that what I am is bound up always with ancestral site" (Alexander 1993, 23).

Mediating self-centralization (or identity through individuation) and sameness with others (collective identity that is identity created through identification with clan) is a post-colonial practice. The constant and continual mediation of the extremes of individual and relational selves, rather than complete identification with one or the other, marks an act of asserting agency. The result is some ever-changing sense of relational individualism.

Western philosophical systems have traditionally considered the self in connection with consciousness; in fact, there is an assumption of subjectivity as conscious-ness. For example, Cartesian dualism and Kantian radical autonomy treat reason as synonymous with conscious reason and consciousness as disembodied or at least as possessing some sort of ability to become disembodied.

The Eastern ideal of selfhood also involves transcending the individual self, the embodied self, and becoming One consciousness— a consciousness shared by all things that exist. The fundamental belief rests upon the radically un-Cartesian assumption that all is One, that it is our inaccurate perceptual apparatus, associated with the body, that inhibits the perception of the relatedness of all beings. Assuming that the perception of this sort of oneness is limited by embodiment is also to assume a mind/body split similar but variant to the mind/body distinction assumed in Western philosophical traditions.

The "identity" of the post-colonial subject that I envision is located in embodied memory. The only constant through discomforting cultural, linguistic, temporal and spatial discontinuity is the body and its memories. I may be a collection of discontinuous multicultural fragments but collection is the imperative. The common connecting element is the memory and the body through which memory is generated and maintained. One may have multiple selves, roles, ways of being, which differ from place to place, but they are all housed in one body and its memories.

Any sense of consistent identity is necessarily bound to embodiment. Western theorists have traditionally sought a sense of self that is permanent over time. But for multicultural nomads there is an additional issue— to search for a sense of self that remains constant in various places. Space rather than time is centralized because for nomadic subjects the temporal discordance that St. Augustine problematized is further complicated by spatial discontinuity. The body is not only a locus of permanence in time because of its enduring overall structure; it is the locus of a type of permanence in time because it is the locus of memory. The past and the future are held together within the present, not as remembered past or anticipated future, but as temporally distinct moments held together via shared place in the present. Experiences that would otherwise fracture continuous experience can coexist in embodied memory.

## CONCLUSION

The person who does not have and act upon conflict has less personal and more socially constructed (a la postmodern) identity. It is through the identification with or opposition to various traditional paradigms and the manipulation of languages and their corresponding conceptual systems that one creates an extended sense of agency, an agency less accessible to those who inhabit any one tradition comfortably.

## Chapter Six

# Beyond Common Ground

## INTRODUCTION

Paradigmatic shifts in philosophy, communications, and conflict resolution, should have a significant impact on counter-terrorism efforts. First, the sender/receiver model of communication has been challenged by a model that locates meaning as taking place in the mind of the receiver rather than being sent "in" the message. Secondly, traditional philosophical models of what constitutes cognition, reason, and the components of ethical deliberation, have been challenged by empirical evidence in the cognitive sciences that has demonstrated that most thinking is unconscious and immediate and consists primarily of metaphorical associations. Third, traditional models of conflict resolution which seek to find common ground between members in a dispute have been challenged by a re-conceptualization of conflict as a result of stories rather than being the result of internal or organic conflicting interests.

## THE LOCATION OF MEANING

The linear model of communication:

Speaker → message → audience

in which the message is *sent* from speaker to audience is outmoded
and replaced with a new model that represents meaning as happen-
ing in the mind of the receiver,

> The problem is that a meaning cannot simply be transferred, like
> a letter mailed from point A to point B. Instead, listener create
> meanings from messages based on factors like autobiography
> history, local context, culture, language/symbol systems, power
> relations, and immediate personal needs" (Corman, Trethewey,
> Goodall, 2008. 156).

We should move away from a communication model in which
the message is something that should retain it's meaning in the
sending process and not get lost in translation. The idea that ideally
the communication arrives intact at its intended destination is not as
strategically strong as a message that has been encoded to trigger
calculated responses in the intended audience. To this idea, which
came out of the Center for Strategic Communication as Arizona
State University, I would add:

1. The audience will put together elements of the message that
   cohere with the story they are a part of and either disregard or
   react against elements that don't cohere with the story the
   audience is a part of.
2. Meaning is continuously reproduced through repetition by
   the audience.
3. The meanings of the message are continually re-constructed.
   In the struggle for meaning production, even if it is possible
   to "win," the victory may be short lived because meaning is
   never stable or fixed although it can be more or less stabilized
   by repetition by the object (audience) of the meaning. If, on
   the other hand, the message is not repeated and re-constructed, it will die. The stability of a narrative over time is
   something we should think about not only in terms of our
   own narrative plans but also in terms of figuring out ways to

undermine the reproduction of terrorist narratives. The undermining will involve new meaning construction. We can't control the dissemination of "their" narrative but we can fiddle with the appropriation and repetition of it.

We can't stop a terrorist narrative from being disseminated. But we can question/undermine/deconstruct the authority of the powers that legitimate it. And further, we can make a better narrative move. What is a "better" narrative move?

A better narrative move is the creation and repetition of not a singular but multiple narrative strands that are more attractive to the identity of the audience.

## METAPHORIC ASSOCIATION
## AS UNCONSCIOUS THOUGHT

Empirical research in cognitive science and cognitive linguistics has demonstrated that the human mind excels at metaphoric association— understanding and experiencing one thing in terms of another. We are *so* good at sorting and sifting and finding cohesive patterns that we make associations between concepts however flawed or helpful the connections is, or however arbitrary or dissimilar. We see examples in everyday life:

Time is money.

Up is good.

Down is bad.

According to Lakoff and Johnson (2003) the one thing we all share as human beings is that we think and act as a result of metaphoric assumptions and thinking is largely unconscious metaphoric association. Our conventional ways of talking presuppose metaphors we are rarely conscious of. Metaphors are not merely words we use. They are an apparatus through which we perceive things and we act accordingly. These notions challenge basic philosophical assumptions by demonstrating that most thought is unconscious (that is, one cannot think very far about the mechanisms of one's own thought in the Lockean fashion), and that abstract concepts are metaphorical rather than literal, "The fundamental role of metaphor is to project inference patterns from source domain to target domain" (Lakoff and Johnson, 1999. 128). The distinction between literal and metaphorical is not a distinction between two types of meaning or reference, but the difference between the familiar and the unfamiliar. These findings alter basic assumptions about the thing we think of as central to humanity— reason. Now we have to think differently about what it is, what it means, to reason.

The second chapter identified persuasive techniques in the terrorist narratives that revealed, among other things, questionable associations:

"Nations are attacking Muslims like people fighting over a plate of food."

"Crusader armies spreading like locusts."[1]

In light of the contributions of recent cognitive science in understanding human cognition (Baumgartner, P. Payr, S. 1995, Gardner, H. 1985, Herman 2003, Hogan 2009, Aldama 2010) and taking into account the model of communication in which meaning isn't sent but created in the receiver's mind, two processes are recommended for improving cross-cultural communication. One process should identify metaphoric assumptions of both or all cultures trying to communicate. If sender and receiver have incompatible metaphorical associations, the meaning created in the mind of the receiver can be very different from what is intended by the sender of the communication. Consider, for example, President Bush's characterization of U.S. efforts to counter terrorism as a "crusade." It is hard to imagine a more counter-productive reference. We need to become as sensitive as we can be about divergent cultural metaphors because we are interested in mis-communication, effects of communication, and what occurs in the mind of receiver. Ultimately, we want to encode messages that have the best possible chance of being well-received.

Secondly, if reasoning is largely based upon culturally available metaphoric prototypes and frames of reference, the strategic possibilities of "triggering" are limited only by unfamiliarity. Triggers in an actual text trigger a virtual text in the receiver's mind. Triggering presuppositions is a way of meaning more, and communicating more, than the text actually says. (Bruner 27– 8).

Table 6.1 illustrates the way triggers operate in creating a reality in the mind of the reader, a reality that is not explicitly stated but implied.

**Table 6.1.  Trigger and Presupposition Examples**

| Trigger | Presupposition |
|---|---|
| John didn't see the dog. | There is a dog. |
| Examples taken from Stormfront.org: | |
| *Trigger* | Presupposition |
| "And there is the issue of what exactly to say." | Something needs to be said. |
| "…the problem with humanity…." | There is a problem with humanity. |
| "I know it isn't fair of the world for Blacks to have been born with such a disadvantage…" | Blacks are at a disadvantage and they were born with it. |
| "We must secure the existence of our people and a future for White children." | The existence of "our people" and White children is in danger. |
| "The attentive reader may wonder how the situation has gotten as grave as it has." | The situation is grave. |

Other forms of triggers are the representation of paradigmatic scenarios. The more paradigmatic the less conscious thought required. Reference to cultural figures, like John Burch, or historical vantage points, like the Crusades, are triggers. Triggers can be symbols like a swastika or a cross.

If we think of thought as instantaneous unconscious metaphoric association then it is possible to think of trigger words, symbols, all

sorts of reference, and most influential of all are storied identification triggers.

Metaphors work underground. And they don't have truth value.
They are neither true nor false. They have what philosophers call
verisimilitude, or they don't. And when they don't, they create it.
Human cognition works to find the similar even in the dissimilar. It
is here that creative possibilities are abundant. It is also here that
the possibilities for manipulation are ripe. A word of caution: terrorists or potential terrorists are not alone in their vulnerability to
triggers. They can be utilized by anyone and are in constant operation. The only panacea is consciousness. We should be as aware of
our own vulnerability to triggers as we are to those of the people we
are trying to communicate with. Above I said that the strategic
possibilities of employing triggers is limited only by cultural unfamiliarity. Diasporic populations, with their access and familiarity
with more than one culture's conceptual systems, are, in fact, better
suited to ironic observations of the incompatibly dissimilar (for
example, incompatible cultural premises) and should be the least
vulnerable to triggers and most capable of one type of conscious
panacea to the triggering of unconscious reference: It is, in Haraway's words,

> about contradictions that don't resolve into larger wholes ...
> about the tension of holding incompatible things together be-
> cause both or all are necessary and true....It is also a rhetorical
> strategy and a political method (Haraway 1991).

Part of understanding our own cultural frames understanding the
non-universality of culturally-specific dichotomies:

- Subjective/objective
- Art/science
- Personal/political
- Imagination/reason
- Irrational/rational

- Meaning/fact
- Metaphorical/literal
- Appearance/reality

Let me flush out one of these dichotomies as a particularly relevant example. Regarding policy, it is not mis-guided to think that it is at the level of personal identity that counter-terrorist strategies may be able to make in-roads (Corman, Trethewey, Goodall, 552). It is, however, misguided to think that distinctions between the two are so universally clear. While personal and cultural identities are not the same thing, the sharp distinction between the two is part of Western conceptual framework that is not universally assumed. Personal and political identities are different "things" but they are not opposite "things". And each has qualities of the other.

The feminist discomfort with the sharp distinction is shared by entire non-Western populations. Gish Jen (2013) describes the differences between Asian and Western approaches to identity and narrative in terms of the differences in conceptions of the self as autonomous or alternatively as "interdependent," defined by social roles and context rather "a modern linear world of conflict and rising action, but rather one of harmony and eternal, cyclical action, in which order, ritual and peace are beauty, and events spell, not excitement or progress but disruption."

## BEYOND COMMON GROUND

In times of conflict perhaps we should consider doing something other than looking for common ground. Perhaps our metaphor:

Conflict resolution = finding common ground

should be reconsidered. There may be certain things that can't be reconciled. Perhaps reconciliation and resolution doesn't have to be the goal. As in Haraway's ironic use of "irony," "our own" narratives ought to be structurally strong enough to accommodate conflict and deep disagreement.

A new approach to conflict resolution pioneered by John Winslade and Gerald Monk focuses on how conflicts are produced by cultural narratives. Winslade and Monk argue that oftentimes what people want, the "interests" that traditional models try to find in common, is not initially internal but is generated by stories they see themselves as a part of and then internalized. Interests are "conditioned" by stories.

Alex Schmid recommends that we need both counter-narratives and alternative narratives. Alternative narratives are essential so that we get ahead of the game and are not always in a reactionary position. As concerns alternative narrative specifically, we should get better at holding incompatible things together. Finding or creating commonality is one move but there are other moves. We should acknowledge difference and get comfortable with it. Consistent with my view that narrative is bigger, better, and more accommodating than the linear, unified structure allows, conflicting narratives can co-exist without being unified, consolidated, or otherwise silenced.

I am suggesting enhancing narrative conflict resolution with an Internarrative model (Maan 2010). Some positions are so incommensurable that seeking common ground may be misguided. Finding common ground may be what the human mind is inclined to do and may be an even stronger inclination for Americans, consistent with a national identity as a "melting pot", but sometimes, and at best, it may not be effective.

## A NEW AMERICAN NARRATIVE FRAMEWORK

Conceptualizing and advertising an American narrative that encompasses difference, even conflict, without being threatened by it is essential. Our narrative should welcome conflict. If we are not conflicted we are not thinking. And if we are not mindful of conflicting narratives then we are not doing what we should be doing:

disseminating a national strategic narrative (Porter and Mykleby, 2011) that locates its identity not in one narrative or another but in the glue that holds multiple narratives together.

The Bush era slogan "war on terrorism" forces one to take sides without any inherent persuasive power to pull an individual or group in one direction or another. The slogan relies on identification as a victim for its persuasive power. But it is a weak narrative; it leaves identification open and vulnerable. Both, or all, sides will identify themselves with the victim and view their actions as consistent with fighting the war on terror. This war relies on an unvoiced assumption that the narrative begins with this current victimization, as the narrative structure is linear rather than cyclical. But in the mind of the "other" this event was not the beginning and if everyone jumps on the linear narrative bandwagon with its attendant need to stabilize a beginning, there will be endless disagreement about when the beginning was. If, on the other hand, the "other" does not share the same structural assumptions, the "other" can exploit this assumption with counter-examples of "beginnings". When we invoke a narrative with a unified structure it is immediately countered in the mind of the "other" and the speaker not only loses credibility but also opens himself up to a litany of counter-examples.

The "war on terror" is the war Al Qaeda thinks of itself as fighting. It is the war white separatists in the U.S. are prepared for. It is a narrative co-opted by right-wing extremists in Europe (Kundnani, 27). An essential narrative strategy of terrorist recruitment is to dichotomize "us" and "them" and then to align "us" with good and "them" with evil, "us" with victim and "them" with the aggressor, "us" as on the side of God and "them" as heathens. Given these dichotomies who wouldn't align themselves with the "us" category? Most people, members of Al Qaeda as well as members of the U.S. Department of Defense will align themselves with the "us" category. Under the "us" category (on both sides of a conflict) will come a long list of historical wrongs inflicted upon "us". This dichotomy is a conceptual trap leaving participants, combatants, if you will, endlessly in conflict about who is "us" and who is "them". No one is going to win that conflict. Both sides of a conflict will always justify violence by reference to a conflict narrative—a war. A counter-terrorism strategy must be a counter-fundamentalist strategy. And the commitment to, and even the unconscious assumption of, linear unified narrative is a brand of fundamentalism.

While the current administration has been careful to refine communication referring to the scope of the conflict and the nature of the threat (away from the "boundless global war on terror" language toward descriptions of "targeted efforts" and "partnerships" with other countries) (Obama, 2013) our national narrative still needs to be developed. A "war of ideas" is a more nuanced description of the situation than a "war on terror" but a "war of ideas" is still a weak metaphor. It is ineffectual. An idea cannot be killed or imprisoned or expelled from the mind or from society. Bad ideas have to be bettered, and in the case of counter-terrorist strategy, they need to be more attractive than the alternative.

I am not simply suggesting replacement of the conflict metaphor with another. Nor am I suggesting that we develop a competing metaphor, even a non-conflict metaphor. I am not suggesting this because it is not necessary. Rather than replacing the conflict metaphor we need to get outside it and encompass it. We, the United States, are already in possession of a metaphor that encompasses conflict. The U.S. already has the advantage here; we *are* the alternative metaphor.

We are an experiment in democracy, an experiment in religious tolerance, an experiment in preserving the dignity of the individual while considering the greatest good for the greatest number. And, as in many experiments, we sometimes make mistakes and we sometimes get results we don't want and didn't expect and then we modify our procedures and try again. As a young culture the U.S.

doesn't have the rigid fixed national identity that some other nations do. We are not so philosophically entrenched that we cannot re-think our intended results and re-calibrate. If we posit our narrative as an imperfect and on-going attempt, we encourage good will (if even grudging). If we posit ourselves as morally or culturally superior, or as victims, we encourage the resuscitation of contrary evidence and we are back in conflict.

We have an advantage over fundamentalist narratives and our advantage didn't come as the result of moral superiority and the advantage does not belong to any particular political party. Our advantage is that long before the events of 9/11 an American narrative has been one of inclusion. An American narrative must carefully avoid mirroring fundamentalist rhetoric by not forcing individuals to make a choice between religious beliefs and nationality. An American narrative enables one to be a Sikh, a Muslim, a Jew, and not be in conflict with those who have other beliefs. Our narratives co-exist. They do not have to harmonize. Forgetting that makes us weak. We play right into the hands of terrorist recruiters when we burn the Koran, when we attempt to silence dissent, and when we adhere to a fundamentalist national narrative.

The United States does not have one narrative theme that must either integrate or silence multiplicity. We do not have one story. There is no one American identity. Our national narrative structure should not reflect singularity, but rather, co-existent multiplicity.

## NOTE

1. While these statements are commonly understood as similes, I refer here to the understanding of simile as a subcategory of metaphor.

# References

## CHAPTER 1

Akerboom, E., National Coordinator for Counter-Terrorism, ed. (2010) *Countering Violent Extremist Narratives*. The Hague: NCTb, Jan. 2010. 9

Alon, N., Omar, H., (2004) "Demonic and Tragic Narratives in Psychotherapy" *Healing Plots: The Narrative Basis of Psychotherapy.* American Psychological Association Press. Washington, D.C.

McAdams, D. (2008) "American Identity: The Redemptive Self," Division One Award Addresses. *The General Psychologist* Vol 43, No. 1.

Obama, B. (May 23, 2013) Remarks by the President at the National Defense University, Fort McNair, Washington, D.C.

Schmid, A.P. (2012) "The Revised Academic Consensus Definition of Terrorism" *Perspectives on Terrorism*, 6, 2.

———. (2014) "Al-Qaeda's 'Single Narrative' and Attempts to Develop Counter-Narratives: the State of Knowledge" International Center for Counter-Terrorism Research paper, The Hague, The Netherlands.

Zalman, A. (2009) "Strategic Communication in Irregular Wars" speech delivered at Strategic Communication for Combating Terrorism Conference. Ankara, Turkey.

## CHAPTER 2

Aristotle, *Poetics*, (1987), Janko, R, trans. Hacket. vii, 26– 33.

Bateson, M, (1990), *Composing a Life*, Plume.

Braidotti, R, (1994), *Nomadic Subjects*, Columbia University Press, 35.

Bruner, J, (1990), *Acts of Meaning*, Harvard University Press.

Casebeer, W and Russell, J, (March 2005), Storytelling and Terrorism: Towards a Comprehensive 'Counter Narrative Strategy', *Strategic Insights,* vol iv, issue 3.

Corman, S, Trethewey, A, Goodall, H.L., Lang, P, eds. (2008) *Weapons of Mass Persuasion*, 88-89.

Goldstein, R, (1989), *The Late Summer Passion of a Woman of Mind*, Farrar, Straus, and Giroux. 57.

Johnson, J, (1993), *Moral Imagination: Implications of Cognitive Science for Ethics*, University of Chicago Press.

Laity, M. (2009) Key note speech delivered Strategic Communication for Combating Terrorism conference, Ankara, Turkey.

Linde, C, (1993), *Life Stories: The Creation of Coherence*, Oxford University Press.

Lloyd, G, (1993), *Being in Time: Selves and Narrators in Philosophy and Literature,* Routledge.

Maan, A, (July 2013), Sneaky Stories: Challenges to Moral Contraband, *Philosophical Practice*, 8, 2, 1201– 1213.

MacIntyre, A, (1981*), After Virtue: A Study in Moral Theory,* University of Notre Dame Press.

McAdams, D, (Spring, 2008), American Identity: The Redemptive Self, *The General Psychologist*, 43, 1.

McAdams and McLean, (June 2013) Narrative Identity*, Current Directions in Psychological Science,* vol. 22, issue 3, 233– 238.

Ricoeur, P, (1995), *Time and Narrative II*, trans. McLaughlin, K. and Pellauer, D. University of Chicago Press.

Ricoeur, P, (1992), *Oneself As Another,* trans. Blamey, K. University of Chicago Press.

Schmid, A. (2014) "Al-Qaeda's 'Single Narrative' and Attempts to Develop Counter-Narratives: The State of knowledge. International Centre for Counter-Terrorism Research paper—The Hague.

Schaffer, R, (1992), *Retelling a Life: Narration and Dialogue in Psychoanalysis*, Harper Collins.

## CHAPTER 3

Black, Don. "Intro Material For People New To Stormfront" www.stormfront.org

Maan, A. (Dec. 2005) "Post-Colonial Practices and Narrative Nomads: Thinking Sikhism Beyond Metaphysics" *Sikh Formations: Religion, Culture, Theory.* Vol.1, number 2. Routledge: UK.

Schmid, A. (2005) "Terrorism as Psychological Warfare" http:// www.academia.edu/3169882/Terrorism_as_Psychological. p.144

Volkan, V. (2012) "September 11 and Societal Regression" http:// www.vamikvolkan.com

Volkan, V. "Suicide Bombers" (2007) www.vamikvolkan.com/suicide-bombers.php.

White, M. and Epston, D. (1990), *Narrative Means to Therapeutic Ends,* Norton: NY

World Islamic Front, "jihad Against Jews and Crusaders" Feb. 23, 1988. Fas.org/irp/world/para/docs/980223-fatwa.htm.

Zalman, A. (summer 2009) "The Global War on Terror: A Narrative in Need of a Rewrite" *Ethics and International Affairs,* Vol.23.2. p. 4– 5.

Zalman, A. (2009) "Strategic Communication in Irregular Wars" Speech delivered at Strategic Communication for Combating Terrorism Conference, Ankara, Turkey.

"Islamism and Language: How Using the Wrong Words Reinforces Islamist Narratives" Quilliam, p. 2.

# CHAPTER 4

Gough, S. (April 7, 2004) "The Evolution of Strategic Influence" US Army War College Strategy Research Project.

Jenkins, B. (March 2, 2006) "Lessons for Intelligence in the Campaign Against al Qaeda" *Vanguard.*

Jenkins, B. (Sept. 8, 2002) San Diego Union Tribune.

Jenkins, B. (June 26, 2005) "Strategy: Political Warfare Neglected" RAND Blog: http://www.rand.org/blog/2005/06/strategy-political-warfare-neglected.html

Schmid, A. (Jan. 2014) "Al-Qaeda's 'Single Narrative' and Attempts to Develop Counter-Narratives: The State of Knowledge." International Centre for Counter-Terrorism Research paper—The Hague p.1.

Spivak, G. (1987) *In Other Worlds: Essays in Cultural Politics,* Routledge: NY.

Philip Taylor. 1999. British Propaganda in the Twentieth Century: Selling Democracy, Edinburgh University Press. In: http;//www.leeds.ac.uk/ics/book-pt2.htm; Oct 1, 2003).

Tiffin, C. and Lawson, A. ed. (1994) "Introduction: The Textuality of Empire" *De-Scribing: Post-Colonialism and Textuality*, London: Routledge. p. 3.

9/11 Commission Report (2004) Washington D.C. Government Printing Office, p. 363.

# CHAPTER 5

Barthes, Roland (1977) "The death of the author"*Image-Music-Text*, edited by Stephen Heath. New York: Hill and Wang.

Cohn, Bernard (1996) *Colonialism and its forms of knowledge.* New Jersey: Princeton University Press.

Derrida, Jacques (1998) *Monolingualism of the Other; or the Prosthesis of Origin.* California: Stamford University Press.

Foucault, Michel (1977) "What is an author? In *Language, Counter-Memory, Practice: Selected Essays and Interviews*, edited by Donald Bouchard. Ithaca: Cornell University Press.

Johnson, Mark (1993) *The Moral Imagination: Implications of Cognitive Science for Ethics.* Chicago: University of Chicago Press.

Kumar, Nita (1994) *Women as Subjects: South Asian Histories.* Charlottesville: University Press of Virginia.

Lakoff, George, and Mark Johnson (1980) *Metaphors We Live By.* Chicago: University of Chicago Press.

Landry, Donna, and Gerald Maclean (1996) *The Spivak Reader.* New York: Routledge.

Maan, Ajit (1999) Internarrative Identity. Rowman and Littlefield, Lanham: NJ.

MacIntyre, Alasdair (1981) *After Virtue.* Indiana: University of Indiana Press.

Olney, James (1980) *Autobiography: Essays Theoretical and Critical.* New Jersey: Princeton University Press.

Quine, W.V. (1951) "The Two Dogmas of Empiricism." *The Philosophical Review* 60: 20–43.

Ricoeur, Paul (1983) *Time and Narrative*, vol. 1. Chicago: University of Chicago Press.

———. 1985. *Time and Narrative*, vol.2. Chicago: University of Chicago Press.

———. 1988. *Time and Narrative*, vol.3. Chicago: University of Chicago Press.

———. 1991. "Narrative Identity" *Philosophy Today* Spring: 73–81.

———. 1992. *Oneself as Another.* Chicago: University of Chicago Press

# CHAPTER 6

Baumgartner, P. and Payr, S. (1995) Speaking Minds: Interviews with Twenty Eminent Cognitive Scientists. Princeton University Press.

Bruner, J. (1986) *Actual Minds, Possible Worlds.* Harvard University Press.

Corman, S. Trethewey, A. and Goodall, H.L. (2008) Weapons of Mass Persuasion: Strategic Communication to Combat Violent Extremism, Peter Lang. N.Y.

Corman , S. Dooley, K. (2009) "Strategic Communication on a Rugged Landscape: Principles for Finding the Right Message" Speech delivered at Strategic Communication For Combating Terrorism Conference. Ankara, Turkey.

Gardner, H. (1985) The Mind's New Science: A History of the Cognitive Revolution. Basic Books: New York.

Haraway, Donna (1991) *Simians, Cyborgs, and Women: The Reinvention of Nature.* Routledge.

Hogan, Patrick, (2009) *Understanding Nationalism: On Narrative, Cognitive Science, and Identity.* Ohio State University Press.

Jen, G. (2013) *Tiger Writing: Art, Culture, and the Interdependent Self.* Harvard University Press.

Johnson, M. (1994) *Moral Imagination: Implications of Cognitive Science for Ethics*, University of Chicago Press.

Kundnani, A. (June, 2012) "Blind Spot? Security Narratives and Far-Right Violence in Europe." Research paper. International Centre for Counter-Terrorism—The Hague. 27.

Lakoff, G. and Johnson, M. (2003) 2nd ed. *Metaphors We Live By,* University of Chicago Press.

Lakoff, G. and Johnson, M. (1999) *Philosophy in the Flesh.* Basic Books: NY.

Maan, A. (2010) *Internarrative Identity: Placing the Self,* Rowman and Littlefield. Lanham, Maryland.

*Narrative Theory and the Cognitive Science*, ed. Davis Herman. (2003) University of Chicago Press.

Obama, B. (May 23, 2013) Remarks by the President at the National Defense University, Fort McNair, Washington, D.C.

Porter, W. and Mykleby, M. (April 2011) "A National Strategic Narrative by Mr. Y" Woodrow Wilson International Center, on-line.

*Toward a Cognitive Theory of Narrative Acts,* ed. Frederick Aldama. (2010) University of Texas Press.

www.ingramcontent.com/pod-product-compliance
Lightning Source LLC
Chambersburg PA
CBHW062044270326
41929CB00014B/2530